Program Modification

W0107247

TABLE OF CONTENTS

ACKNOWLEDGEMENTS

I must express my thanks to all those who helped in the development of this book, and in particular to Michel Gautier of the Banque Nationale de Paris; to Jean-Pierre Genestier and Jean-Paul Lornage of AFPA; and to Alain Coulon, Michel Dambrine, Brendan M. Flanagan, Pierre Henri Petit, and Jean Claude Utter of Cii-Honeywell Bull. I am indebted to the programmers of the data processing department at Bazar de l'Hotel de Ville for their participation in the first course on program modification.

Nicole Lemelle of the Cii Honeywell Bull Data Processing Logic department prepared the manuscript. The translation is by Ed Troupe of Cii Honeywell Bull.

PROGRAM MODIFICATION

Jean-Dominique Warnier

Cii Honeywell Bull

Part 1

THEORY

1 — INTRODUCTION

THE PROGRAMMER-ANALYST'S ROLE

The pages that follow are based on observation, over the past few years, of the work done by programmer-analysts. Although they come from a wide variety of backgrounds, and are trained in a variety of ways, they seem with rare exception to have at least two things in common.

- They have been trained to create, to organize new data structures, new programs. As a result they tend to regard the development of new projects as their principle job, and accept only with reluctance so-called maintenance work, for which hardly anyone volunteers.
- They have received no training at all in how to modify and develop existing programs and data structures. Programmers assigned to maintenance tasks come to consider their role as minor, their work tedious, and sometimes take such an assignment as an invitation to seek a job elsewhere.

It is only natural that people take little interest in work for which they have not been trained. If we examine the curriculum of courses for beginning or for experienced data processing personnel, we find in fact that training concentrates exclusively on program design and data file organization, to the detriment of modification and development.

It should be added that we have done no better in this regard than anybody else. In the books we have published on programming logic, nearly every example and every exercise has to do with the creation of new programs. In contrast, the experience of recent years has shown us that the majority of programmers and analysts trained in LCP have, upon leaving our courses, been put to work on the modification and correction of existing programs.

It is important to distinguish between maintenance properly speaking, which consists in the correction of errors not detected during the initial testing of a program; and modification, which satisfies new requests from the program's end users. Program maintenance, in the sense defined here, should practically disappear with the proper use of LCP, the Logical Construction of Programs.

We will show, in the following pages, that use of this method alone permits the systematic definition of a set of tests which performs an exhaustive check on program logic.

It then becomes necessary to rethink the distribution of work in a data-processing service. The burden of program design should become lighter, and that of program maintenance very nearly disappear, to the advantage of work on program modification. This change is the only way in which the service can respond to the ever-changing needs of the business it serves. It is a change which presumes a corresponding change in the mentality of programmer-analysts, particularly where it comes to the criteria by which the quality of program modifications is judged.

These criteria are most commonly classed, in descending order of importance, as follows.

- Speed with which the modification is made.
- Reliability of the modification.
- Logical quality of the modification (for future update).

To respond to the real needs of business, we think this order should be reversed.

- Logical quality.
- Reliability.
- Speed of implementation.

For the third point, planning is required. An acceptable schedule can be achieved if program modification takes over from program maintenance. It is essential that end users appreciate the importance of their contribution to the establishment of such a schedule.

What has been said so far makes evident the necessity, in preparing the programmer-analyst for his true role, of having him study program modification, and of having him work through numerous exercises in this area. Courses to which we have given this emphasis have produced good results; but they have lacked written support. This book is intended to furnish students and instructors with such support, the indispensable complement to existing books in LCP.

The reader will find, in the first part, three main chapters:

- An introduction explaining the increasing role of program modification in the workload of data processing services.
- A second chapter showing the way in which the principles of programming logic are applied in the modification of programs designed according to this same logic.
- A third chapter showing how these same logical principles can be applied to the maintenance of empirically-designed programs.

The second part of the book is devoted to exercises, either in the design or in the modification of programs, followed by solutions. This part is intended to give the teacher as well as the student the means to train himself in the subjects developed here.

THE EVOLUTION OF DATA

To understand the necessity for program and data evolution, we must pause for a moment to look at the evolution of the business itself. Any business can be regarded as a system which receives from the outside world the means to produce results for the outside world.

- Changes in the needs of this outside world produce a constant change in the aims of the business, which must respond with new ways of doings things to produce new results.
- Changes in the needs of the business itself are a second spur to evolution.

The evolving functions of the business are ordered by men. These orders constitute the output of a second system: the system of management, a system of decision. This system has as its input the sources of information available to man.

- Facts and events directly perceived.
- Data and information coded in an intelligible language.

We can define information as the representation in the mind of man of the world which surrounds him; and data as the representation, in code, of information. It is by means of data that men communicate with one another. Data constitute the input and the output of a third system, the information system. This system has the function of transmitting data in time and in space, as well as the transformation of data.

These considerations cause us to emphasize the necessity of highly evolutionary information systems, which constantly tend to reduce the distance between the facts and the data intended to represent the facts. When an information system is automated, the differences between fact and data are reduced by the speed of the computer. Their manufacturers strive, in this area as in that of data storage and transmission, to provide an ever-improving service to the user. Such efforts, however, will never in themselves suffice to solve the problem. It is the user himself who must conceptualize data sets and programs which are permanently capable of being modified; and it is the educator who must prepare the programmer-analyst for his principal role: to assure the constant evolution of the logical organization of data and of programs.

The empiricism which has guided (and still too often guides) programmers and analysts in their work results in solutions which are sometimes very sophisticated and elaborate, but which are extremely difficult to modify. As a result, after a few modifications one is obliged to take up the problem all over again to find a new solution. This process, very costly, is both slow and inefficient. To disentangle oneself from such a situation, one must:

- Create clear and easily-modified data processing solutions.
- Train programmers and analysts both technically and psychologically to recognize that their essential role is as much (or more) to make solutions evolve as to invent new solutions.

In the pages that follow, we will try to show how one can make programs evolve. We think (and experience confirms our belief) that it is often less costly to rewrite a program than to attempt to modify an empirical solution. We will, however, try to show how such programs can be modified when time constraints prevent starting over from the beginning.

Above all, we wish to show how an LCP program should be modified; and to make it possible for the user, with the exercises in Part 2, to train himself in LCP program modification.

We are convinced that the workload in designing programs is bound to decrease in data processing services, relative to the work done in intelligent program evolution. We think this is a step forward, a step possible only if programs are designed respecting the principles of data-processing logic.

APPROACHES TO PROGRAMMING

Since machines have come into existence capable of performing logical choices (tabulators, calculators, and later, computers) analysts responsible for the organization of data have approached their work in one of two ways:

- Either by working in an empirical manner;
- Or by using methods designed to define modules or elementary structures from which programs are constructed.

In parallel with the latter approach, we have sought to show how to organize data and programs in hierarchically structured sets.

We will try to present these three approaches so as to find out how to modify programs of various categories. This depends first on the organization of input and output data.

An empirical organization is obtained by tackling the problem at the beginning and working on through to the end. In the past, such an organization was typically produced by the programmer who, having heard the statement of the problem, takes out coding sheets and starts writing instructions.

It is also typified by flowcharts which, using standard symbols, have the peculiarity that some symbols stand for a long series of instructions, while others represent a single instruction. Why? It seems that the use of flowcharts comes from a general awareness of the necessity of summarizing the program; but the importance attached to one instruction rather than another appears more a matter of the programmer's subjective concerns than of the objective logic of the program.

Empirical programs, although sometimes very effective, are for the most part difficult for anyone but their authors to understand. Often enough, even the author himself, coming to his solution some time later, finds it difficult to follow his own program. Empirical programs are hard to modify.

The use of methodical programming has real advantages over empirical programming. Our aim here is not to present the various existing methods, but to point out certain features of the best methods so as to examine the problems in modifying programs designed according to their principles.

Users of these methods seek to list in an orderly fashion the functions which the program is to perform. They study separately the processing of each function, and the programming of the instructions which permit it to be executed. Such programs, more clearly structured than empirical programs, are more easily modified: if a given function is to be changed, one rewrites only the coding which supports the function.

There are, however, certain features common to both approaches which constitute obstacles to program evolution.

- The program as data file is not clearly distinguished from the program as a series of actions.
- More emphasis is placed on languages and techniques than on logic.
- Organization of output and input data for the program is usually totally neglected.
- No definition as mathematical set is given for input and output data, or for program data.

As a result, these methods do not furnish the programmer with the means of dealing with problems in a rigorous and hierarchical manner, since he has neither a definition of sets, nor any precise criteria of subdivision. It seems to us that such tools are necessary to allow later implementation of requested changes under optimum conditions. The approach we recommend consists in the organization of data, and particularly program data, in hierarchical mathematical sets.

In the following chapter, we will follow a review of this approach with a definition of the principles which should govern program modification.

2 — LCP PROGRAM EVOLUTION

LCP PROGRAMS

There is sometimes a resemblance between certain solutions obtained by one or another method, and the organization we propose. However, to arrive at this organization using LCP (Logical Construction of Programs) a certain number of frequently-neglected principles must be respected, and a process of problem resolution used which is radically different from those in normal use.

We must emphasize the importance of this process, for it permits all the logical operations of program modification. It is based on the following postulate:

Any collection of data constitutes one or more sets, which must be mathematically defined.

In this way it is possible to know what to do, and what to do it to.

If we consider a data set, taking 'set' in its mathematical meaning, we must define it:

- By establishing a definition, i.e. by giving all characteristics which allow us to assign an element to the set.
- By establishing a list naming all the elements that make up the set.

Having defined all data sets in the collection, it becomes possible to perform operations on them, establish relationships, etc.

In summary, any logical problem in data processing can be reduced to the definition and ordering of an unknown set from one or more known sets.

To build a program, one must establish the hierarchical organization of the set of output data, then that of the set of input data, from which is deduced the set PI of the logical sequences (1) in a program.

This does not mean that there is only one solution to any given problem but that whatever solution is adopted for the required task is entirely independent of techniques and languages.

The set of logical sequences PI having been defined, the program must then be redefined as the set of instructions Pi.

This set Pi having been defined, it must be brought into relation with the set PI. The act of doing so constitutes the detailed organization of the program. In mathematical terms, set Pi maps to set PI, i.e.

---

1. A logical sequence is an ordered set of instructions executed the same number of times at the same point in the program to process a defined set of data.

each instruction i in set Pi corresponds to one and only one logical sequence s in set PI. In boolean notation:

   i ε s

Instructions must finally be coded in the appropriate language: COBOL, FORTRAN, BASIC, PL/1, assembler, etc. It is of course necessary to take into account the technical environment of the program, and to know thoroughly the language used in writing the program; but technical concerns should only intervene after resolution of the logical problem.

To sum up, the solution of the logical problem of program construction takes place in three steps;

- **Organization into logical sequences, i.e. the complete definition of set PI. This stage is totally independent of technical considerations.**
- **Extensive definition of set Pi by a list of instructions by category.**
- **Ordering the instruction list so that set Pi maps to set PI.**

If the second step takes place before the first step is complete, i.e. a list of instructions is made before the logical sequences have been determined, the logical structure of the program is obscured.

For any given description of the physical input and output files to be processed, and of the procedures to be applied to the input (which together often form the statement of the problem) logical analysis shows that there exist, depending on the case, one or more definitions of the set PI. We will see how the definition of the set PI allows us, in modifying a program, to distinguish modifications in logic from modifications to instructions.

We will also see the usefulness of the 'null set' concept. Empty sets are as indispensable for logical operations on set PI as the zero is for arithmetic operations to any base.

On the subject of null sets, it should be noted that an empty sequence in a program can correspond to a non-empty subset of data. If the mapping of set Pi to set PI has been verified, but there is an element of PI which has no corresponding element in Pi, that element of PI is an empty sequence for which no treatment is required. When a modification is requested, it may be that program logic remains unchanged: a certain number of instructions are to be removed, changed, or added. Some sequences, previously empty, now contain instructions; other sequences now become empty.

The objective, in resolving a problem, is to organize a program which is optimized, and easily modified. Program optimization consists in avoiding all unnecessary branches. Clarity and ease of modification come from complete definition of the set PI. Once this set is ordered, each sequence (i.e. element of PI) is defined as a function of the organization of the input data. The hierarchical organization of the data and of the program allows the isolation of subsets to be modified by identifying the branch of the tree structure in which one is to work.

If the hierarchical organization of data is neglected in programming, branches multiply because the instructions which treat a given subset of the data have not been correctly brought together. The same tests have to be repeated several times. Certain language elements and programming techniques, such as the creation of variables, serve to mask the drawbacks of such procedures; the program remains complicated, heavy, and awkward to change because it is difficult to see what instructions are affected by a requested modification.

In fact, the sole justification for creating pointers, indexes, and variables is that the program involves several phases of processing, i.e. when the elements of certain data sets to be processed are introduced without the criteria of their indentification. The presence of such phases is clear only if input, output, and program data have been subjected to hierarchical analysis. This analysis shows that any subset, at whatever level, is included in the set of the level immediately above, and that all subsets at the same level are disjoint, i.e. have no element in common.

If a subset of instructions corresponds to several logical sequences, it can either be duplicated as needed, or be written as a subroutine independent of the main program, which is reduced to a series of call instructions.

MODIFICATION OF LCP PROGRAMS

We will now study the modification of programs written as we recommend, respecting the rules of logic in the design of data sets. To begin with, it should be noted that modifications may have no effect on program logic. If input data remain unchanged and only the output is modified, the set PI may remain unchanged while the set Pi is altered.

If the hierarchical organization of the set of input data is changed, whether or not the set of output data is altered, the set PI of logical sequences must be redefined, and the set Pi of instruction updated. In other words, any redefinition of PI, the set of logical sequences in the program, implies a redefinition of Pi, the set of instructions; but the reverse is not true.

When modifications are requested, the first concern of the programmer should be to determine whether the set of input data (or the data set input to each program phase) has been changed or not:

- If so, the logic of the program is to be modified.
- If not, in many cases only the content of the logical sequences need be re-examined.

Where program modification involves only the modification of the set Pi, the sequence or sequences involved are identified and updated by deletion, modification, or addition of instructions; the mapping between the new set Pi and the unchanged set PI is then checked. To check the validity of the solution, the Logical Output File (LOF) must be modified as well.

Where program modification has an effect on program logic, it is necessary to:

- **Modify the LOF as needed.**
- **Modify the Logical Input File (LIF).**
- **See whether the modification results in creation of new processing phases or in the alteration of data input to existing phases; if so, modify the organization of input data to these phases.**
- **Review any truth tables affected.**
- **Redefine the set PI.**
- **Redefine the set Pi and check its mapping with PI.**
- **Check the program against the LOF and then debug the program.**

These operations, which can be extensive, allow the production of new solutions which are perfectly clear and which perform well. After modification, the program and its documentation are as well organized as they would be for a new application. Consequently, there is no reason to destroy an old program to make a new one where modifications are extensive. In this situation, the work of producing new programs occupies a decreasing proportion of the total programming workload; and the rigorous principles that govern the redefinition of a program make this the 'noblest' part of the programmer-analyst's work.

To illustrate what we have been saying, let us take an example from the end of the book, 'Logical Construction of Programs', to see how a program can be modified.

Example: a problem in the updating of a stock of merchandise, with automatic re-ordering when the supply of any given item falls below a minimum.

Program Diagram

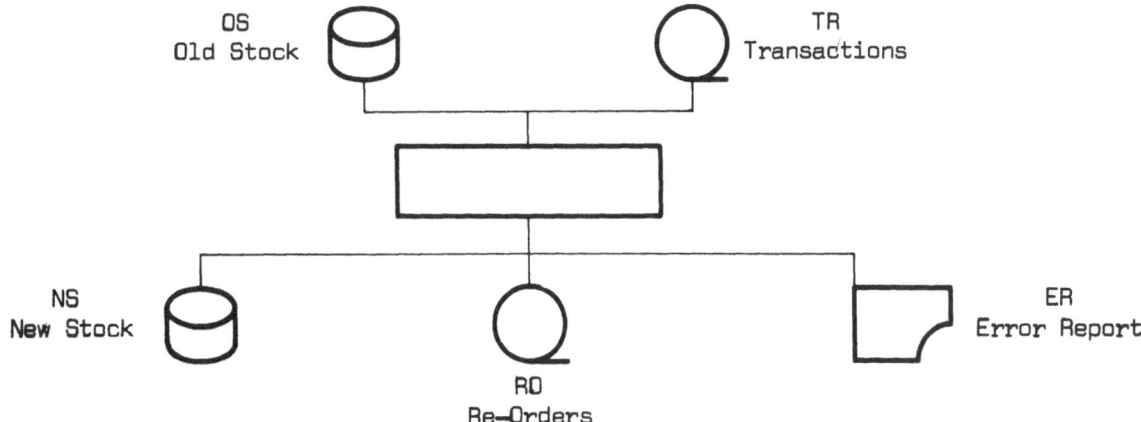

Output Data

- **File NS, New Stock** (0 or 1 record per product)

Product—Number (NrNS)	Quantity (QNS)	Max—Stock	Min—Stock

- **File RO, Re-Orders** (0 or 1 record per product)

Product—Number (NrRO)	Quantity—Reordered (QRO)

- **File ER, Error Report** (0 or 1 record per product)

Product—Number (NrER)	Error—Message (MSG)

Input Data

- **File OS, Old Stock** (0 or 1 record per product) processed sequentially in ascending product-number order.

Product—Number (NrOS)	Quantity (QOS)	Max—Stock	Min—Stock

- **File TR, Transactions** (0 to n records per product) sorted in ascending product-number order.

Product—Number (NrTR)	Quantity [+/—] (QTR)

The 'Quantity' value in Old Stock (QOS), checked beforehand, cannot be less than the corresponding 'Min-Stock' value.

There is an error condition:

- If there is no Old Stock record for the product ($\overline{OS}$).
- If, after calculation, the 'Quantity' value is less than zero (QNS < 0).

Where there is an error, no New Stock record is produced.

Processing

- If OS.$\overline{TR}$, then QNS = QOS.
- If OS.TR, then QNS = QOS +/— QTR, taking an algebraic sum.
- If QNS < Q Min-Stock . $\overline{QNS < 0}$, then calculate QRO = Max-Stock — QNS.

• If QNS < Q Min-Stock . QNS < O, then take QNS as = O and
  QRO = Q Max-Stock.

Output Data Description

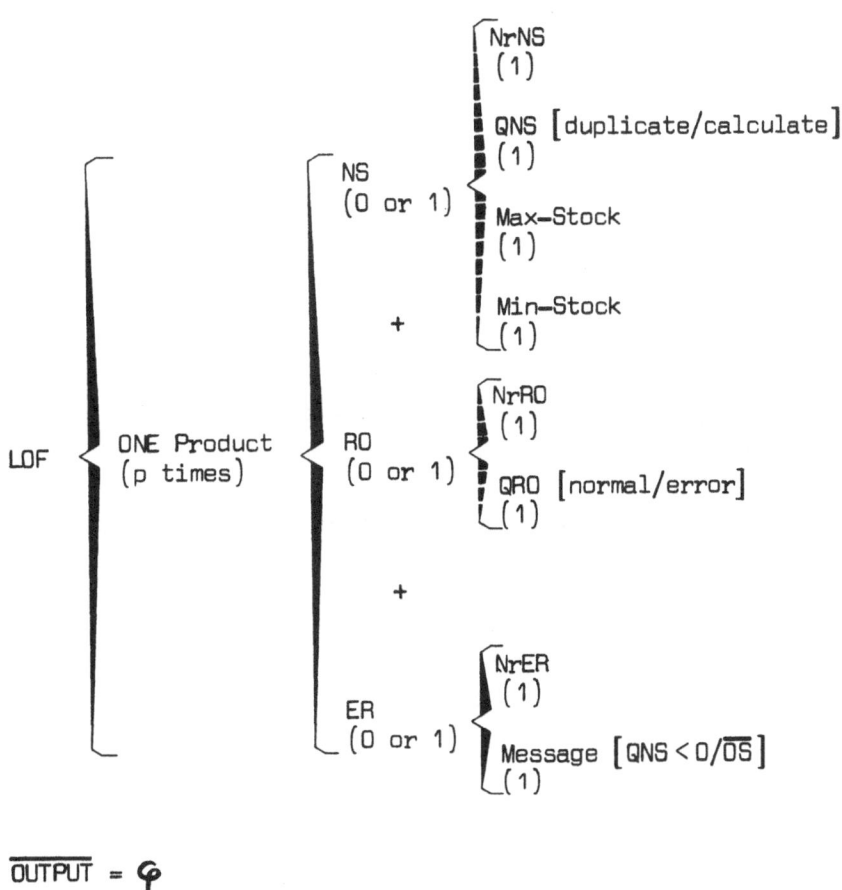

$$\overline{\text{OUTPUT}} = \varphi$$

The sign + is used by convention at the second level of the Logical Output File (LOF) even though NS and ER are mutually exclusive, because an NS record may be produced at the same time as an RO record, and an RO record at the same time as an ER record.

Input Data Description

$$\text{LIF} \left\{ \text{ONE Product} \atop (p\ \text{times}) \right\} \left\{ {\text{OS} \atop (0\ \text{or}\ 1)} + {\text{TR Group} \atop (0\ \text{or}\ 1)} \left\{ \text{ONE Transaction} \atop (t\ \text{times}) \right. \right.$$

In the processing phase, the value 'Quantity' in NS (QNS) establishes a criterion by which we may identify the set to which the data for a given product belongs.

- The set of data for products on which there is an error.
- The set of data for products for which a re-order is required.
- The set of data for products for which a New Stock record is required.

Input Data Description for the Processing Phase (partial output of phase 1)

$$\begin{array}{l} \text{LPF 2} \\ \text{Universal set :} \\ \text{ONE Product OS.TR} \end{array} \left\{ \begin{array}{c} \text{QNS } [<0\ :\ 0\ \text{or}\ 1] \\ + \\ \text{QNS } [<\text{QMin-Stock}\ :\ 0\ \text{or}\ 1] \end{array} \right.$$

Truth Table 1 for Product Data Set

ONE Product OS TR	ER $\overline{\text{OS}}$	OS into NS PUT NS	Calculate QNS See Table 2	Process TR Group
0 0	φ	φ	φ	φ
0 1	X			X
1 0		X		
1 1			X	X

Truth Table 2 for OS.TR Product Data Set

Let N = QNS $\overline{< 0}$; and R = QNS < QMin-Stock.

| ONE OS.TR Product | | PUT | NS < 0 ER | PUT |
N	R	NS	0 in QNS	RO
0	0	φ	φ	φ
0	1		X	X
1	0	X		
1	1	X		X

Having described the data and set up truth tables, we can now establish the hierarchical organization of the program, taking care not to forget the initial processing of the input records to determine the product-number of the first product treated.

Subdivision into Logical Sequences

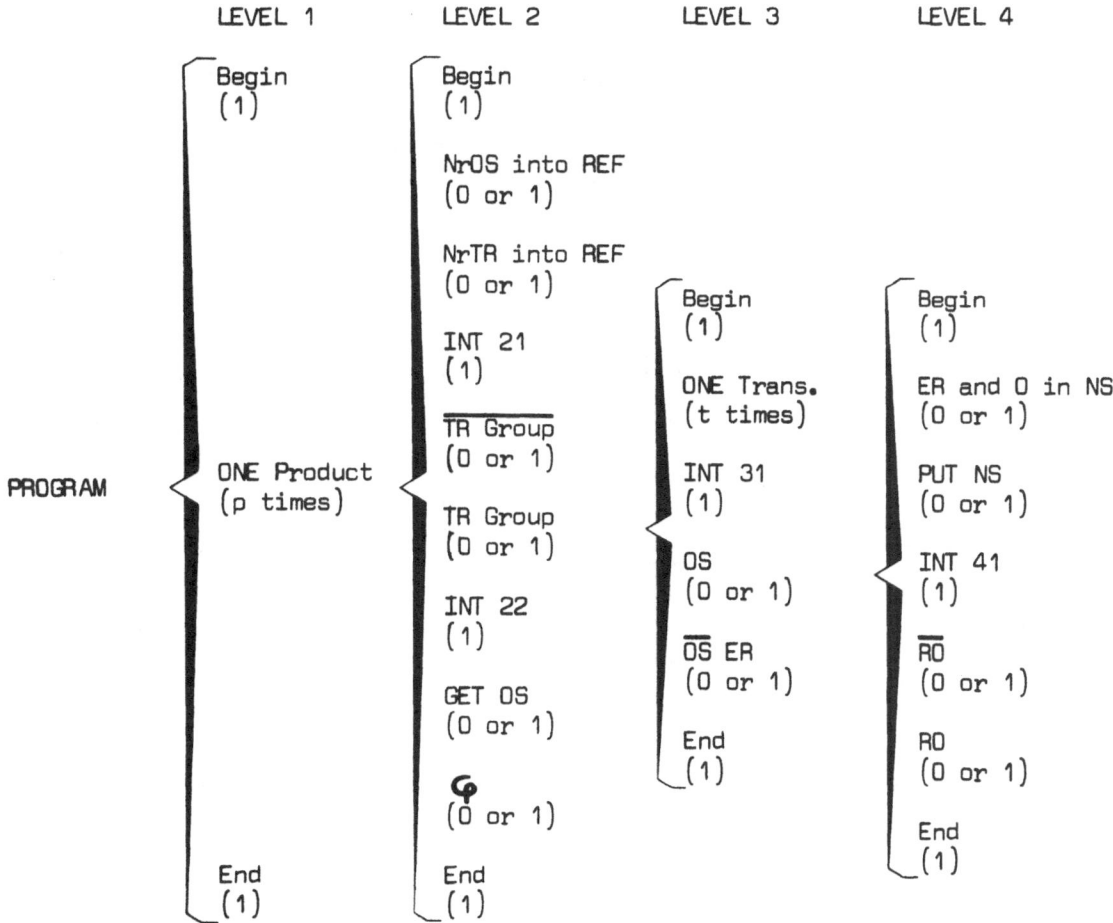

Logical Sequence Flowchart

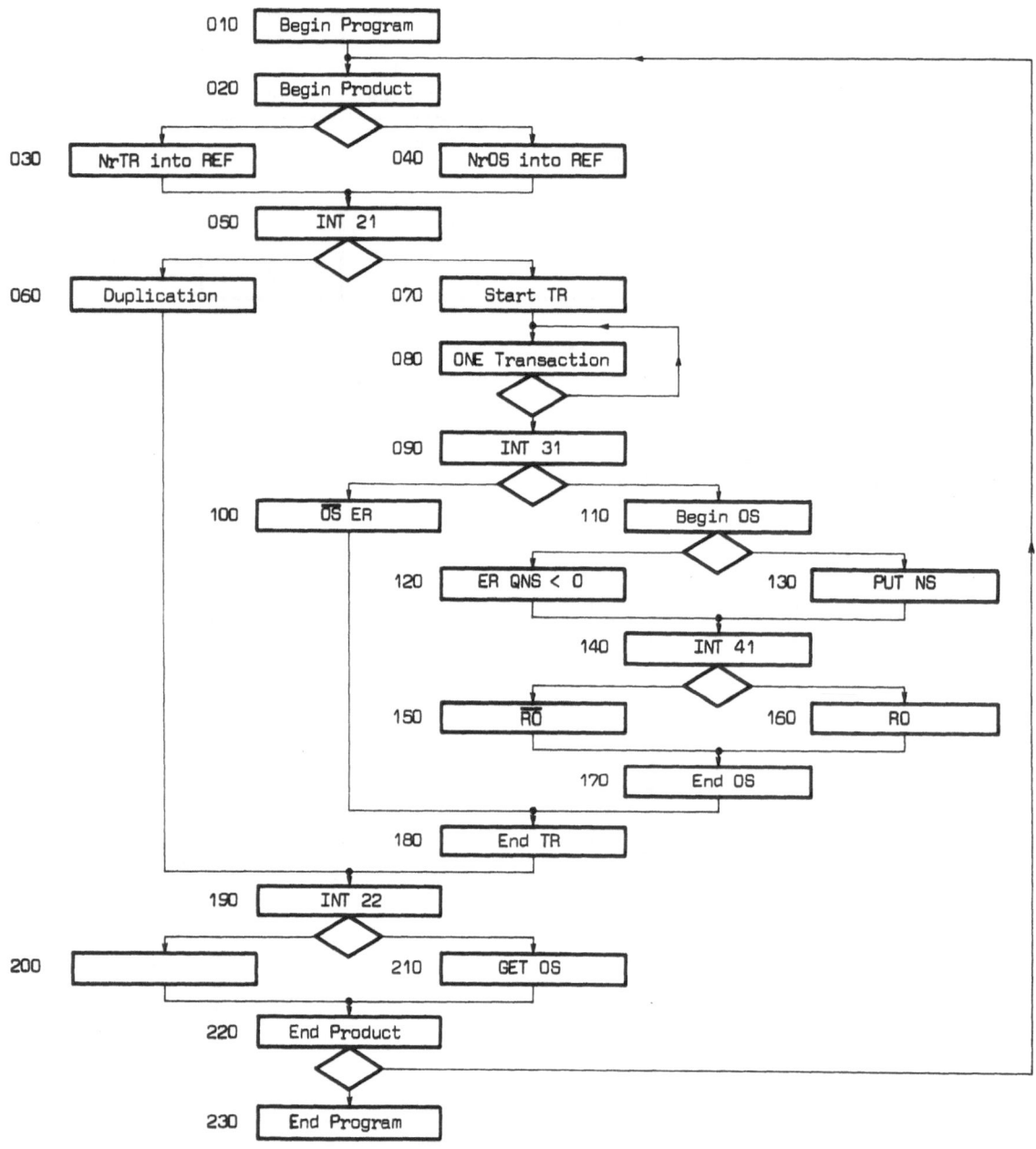

Having established the list of instructions by category, and having checked the mapping of set Pi to set PI, instructions can be sequenced for coding in the chosen language.

Ordered List of Program Instructions

010	GET 1st OS	
	GET 1st TR	
020	IF NrOS $<$ NrTR	040
030	NrTR into REF	050
040	NrOS into REF	
050	IF NrTR = NrREF	070
060	FMT NS	
	PUT NS	190
070	ΣQTR = 0	
080	ΣQTR + QTR	
	GET TR	
	IF NrTR = NrREF	080
090	IF NrOS = NrREF	110
100	FMT $\overline{OS}$ MSG	
	PUT ER & INIT	180
110	QNS = QOS + ΣQTR	
	IF QNS $\overline{< 0}$	130
120	QNS = 0	
	FMT QNS $<$ 0 MSG	
	PUT ER & INIT	140
130	FMT NS	
	PUT NS	
140	IF QNS $<$ QMin-Stock	160
150		170
160	QRO = QMax-Stock — QNS	
	FMT RO	
	PUT RO	
170		
180		
190	IF NrOS = NrREF	210
200		220
210	GET OS	
220	IF $\overline{EOF.OS}$ + $\overline{EOF.TR}$	020
230		End

The preceding pages document the program: statement of the problem, logical files, truth tables, hierarchical program structure, flowchart of logical sequences, and ordered list of program instructions. Use of this documentation permits us to perform the modifications that will be requested.

We will study in succession the various types of possible modifications, illustrating them in terms of this program. In two of the types, only the Logical Output File is changed; no change takes place in the Logical Input File or the Logical Phase File. However, we must check that any new action appearing in the truth table has no effect on data subsets for which there was no action in the original program.

For correct program modification, the following rules apply.

Any modification of files used at the beginning of the first phase of a program or at the beginning of any subsequent phase requires the modification of the set PI of logical sequences in the program, and consequently that of the set Pi of program instructions.

Any modification of output files in a program (either the LOF or the LPF considered as output of the preceding phase) requires the modification of the set Pi of instructions in the program; plus:

- **If the program is derived from truth tables, and if the actions required for new output have an effect on table data subsets which do not correspond to an existing sequence, the set PI must be modified.**

- **Otherwise, set PI remains unchanged.**

First example: no modification to set PI of logical sequences.

The statement of the problem resolved by the preceding program is altered to specify that, in addition to the existing outputs, a report is to list current stock status, with one line per product found in the file NS. For each product, the product number is to be listed, along with the quantity in old stock, the algebraic sum of current transactions, and the quantity in new stock.

New Program Diagram

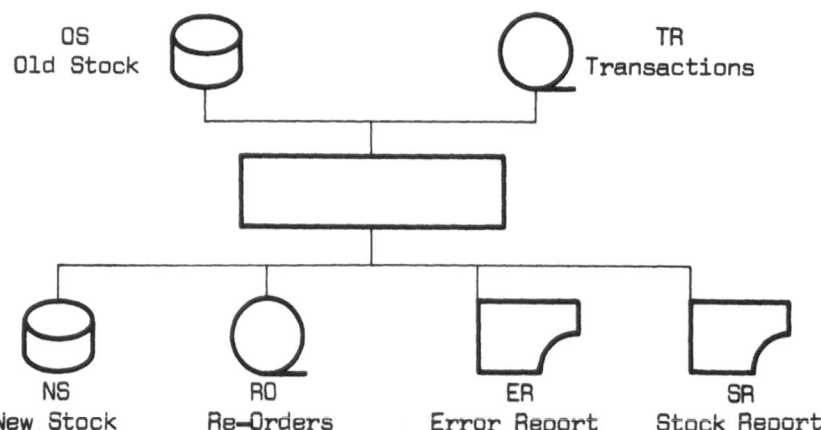

OS
Old Stock

TR
Transactions

NS
New Stock

RO
Re–Orders

ER
Error Report

SR
Stock Report

Stock Report Format

Product—Number (NrSR)   (QOS)   (QNS)

Transactions (ΣQTRSR)

One line per product for which a record is produced in the file NS; where a product is duplicated, spaces are to be printed in the QTRs field.

Resolution of the problem.

1. Modification of the Logical Output File (LOF).

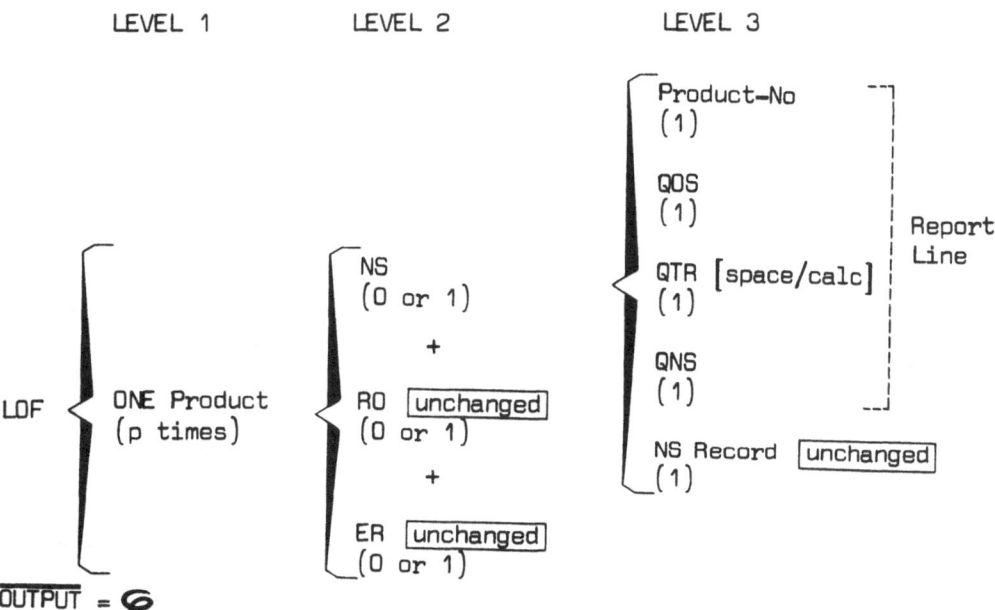

Modification is performed by finding in the tree structure the set to be changed: in this case, the set NS. Note that the LOF must be redrawn to allow for new modifications later on.

2. Table Modification.

The print-report action has to be added to the first table, where it affects a subset of products.

ONE Product OS TR	ER $\overline{\overline{OS}}$	OS into NS Spaces into ΣQTRSR PUT SR, NS	CALC QNS and Σ QTR See Table 2	Process TR Group
0 0	φ	φ	φ	φ
0 1	X			X
1 0		X		
1 1			X	X

This action is to be performed on a subset of products handled in phase 2. It must be present in the second table as well.

ONE OS.TR Product N R	PUT NS & SR	ER NS < 0 0 into QNS	PUT RO
0 0	φ	φ	φ
0 1		X	X
1 0	X		
1 1	X		X

In the first table, output of the Stock Report is performed for the same data subset to which the action of duplication is applied. In the second table, Report output is performed for the same data subset as that processed in the output of NS. As a result:

• The set PI is unchanged.

• The same subroutine may be used to format and print the Stock Report that formats and writes the NS record.

Redefinition of the set Pi involves adding the following instructions:

```
060  Spaces into ΣQTRSR
110  FMT ΣQTR
060  CALL subroutine  NS
130  CALL subroutine  NS
```

Subroutine NS:

    FMT NrSR, QOS, QNS
    PUT SR & INIT
    FMT NS Rec
    PUT NS

To permit future modification, the ordered list of program instructions must be updated to maintain the accuracy of program documentation.

010	GET 1st OS	
	GET 1st TR	
020	IF NrOS < NrTR	040
030	NrTR into REF	050
040	NrOS into REF	
050	IF NrTR = NrREF	070
060	Spaces into ΣQTRSR	
	CALL subroutine NS	190
070	$\Sigma QTR = 0$	
080	$\Sigma QTR + QTR$	
	GET TR	
	IF NrTR = NrREF	080
090		
	IF NrOS = NrREF	110
100	FMT ER.$\overline{OS}$ MSG	
	PUT ER & INIT	180
110	FMT ΣQTR	
	QNS = QOS + ΣQTR	
	IF QNS $\overline{< 0}$	130
120	QNS = 0	
	FMT ER.QNS < 0 MSG	
	PUT ER & INIT	140
130	CALL NS subroutine	
140	IF QNS<QMin-Stock	160
150		170
160	QRO = QMax-Stock − QNS	
	FMT RO	
	PUT RO	
170		
180		
190	IF NrOS = NrREF	210
200		220
210	GET OS	
220	IF $\overline{EOF.OS}$ + $\overline{EOF.TR}$	020
230		End

S/R	FMT NrSR, QOS, QNS PUT SR & INIT FMT NS record PUT NS

Second example: modification of the data set input to the program.

Any change in the organization of input data requires the redefinition of the set PI of logical sequences in the program. The example we have chosen calls for considerable changes in PI, since the data set is altered at a high level for the introduction of a new input file.

Starting with the program we have just modified, we now have a new change to make: data input is to include a file of Cancelled Products, file CP. The file consists of one record per product to be withdrawn from the catalogue.

New Program Diagram

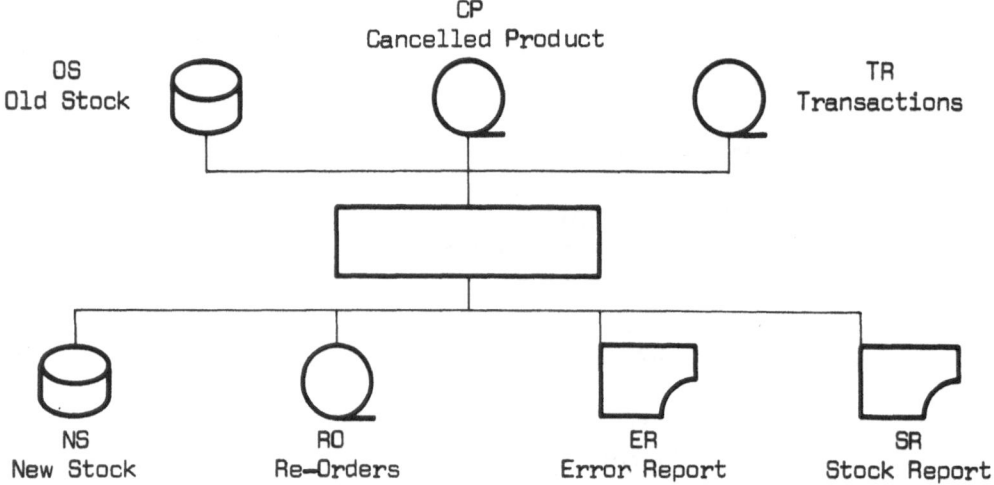

Cancelled-Product (CP) Format (0 or 1 record per product)

Product–Number (NrCP)

If a CP product is found in the Old-Stock file OS, no output results; if there is no corresponding OS record, there is an error (ER CP). In the case where there are transactions for a cancelled product, the transactions must still be read.

Because of the output of error messages for the ER.CP error, the **Logical Output File** must be redefined.

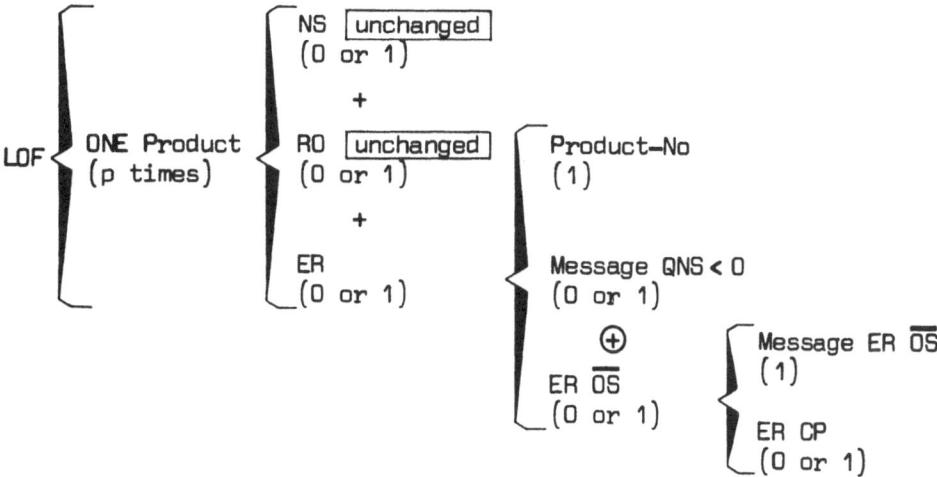

The set $\overline{\text{OUTPUT}}$, formerly null, is also modified: $\overline{\text{OUTPUT}}$ = CP.OS.

Here is the new **Logical Input File.**

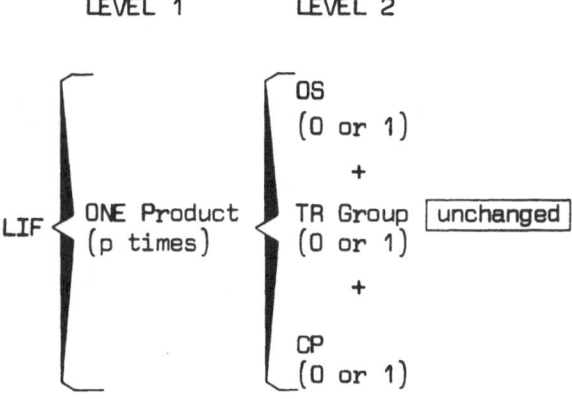

Because of the modification in LIF at Level 2, the corresponding truth table must be changed.

ONE Product OS TR CP	ER $\overline{OS}$	OS into NS Spaces into ΣQTRSR PUT SR, NS	CALC ΣQTR, QNS See T2	ER CP	CNCL
0 0 0	ᚼ	ᚼ	ᚼ	ᚼ	ᚼ
0 0 1	X			X	
0 1 0	X				
0 1 1	X			X	
1 0 0		X			
1 0 1					X
1 1 0			X		
1 1 1					X

Veitch Diagram

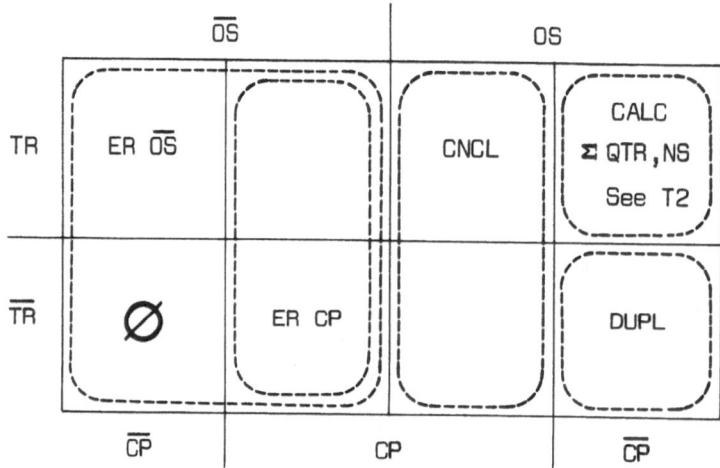

We can now prepare the new program solution, based on the table.

$$
\begin{aligned}
\text{CNCL} &= \text{OS.CP} \\
\text{DUPL} &= \text{OS}.\overline{\text{CP}}.\overline{\text{TR}} \\
\text{CALC } \Sigma\text{QTR, NS} &= \text{OS}.\overline{\text{CP}}.\text{TR} \\
\text{ER OS} &= \overline{\text{OS}} \\
\text{ER CNCL} &= \overline{\text{OS}}.\text{CP}
\end{aligned}
$$

Now it becomes possible to reorganize the program. Because of the new input file CP, the search for the lowest product-number must also be modified.

Logical Sequences

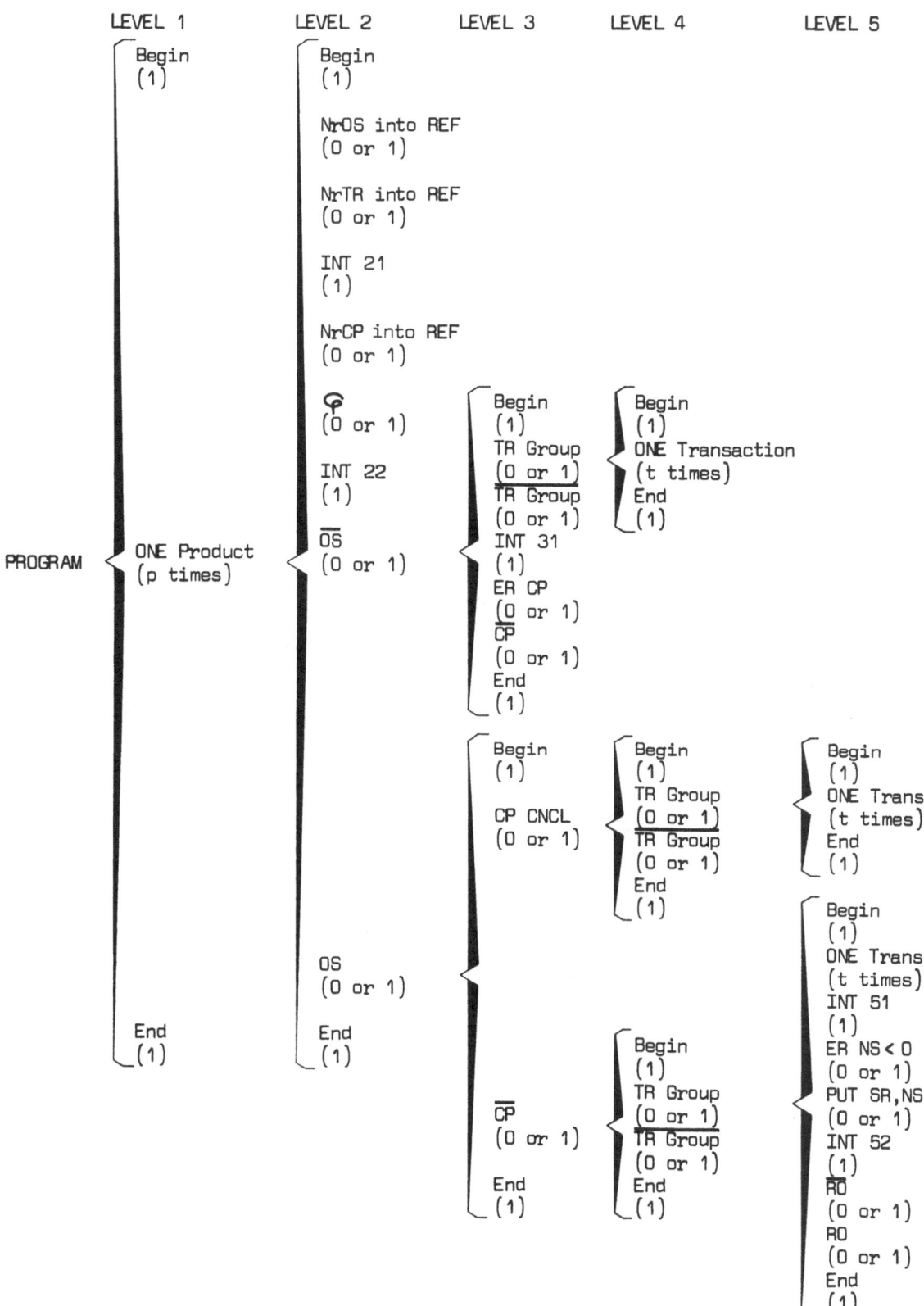

The solution proposed here is not the only valid possible solution. It would take too much time and space to provide equally interesting alternatives; we suggest the reader find these alternative solutions for comparison.

Here is the logical sequence flowchart. Since it no longer fits on one page, we have divided it into two parts:

- Flowchart of the full program.
- Flowchart of the subset OS.$\overline{CP}$.

Flowchart of the full program

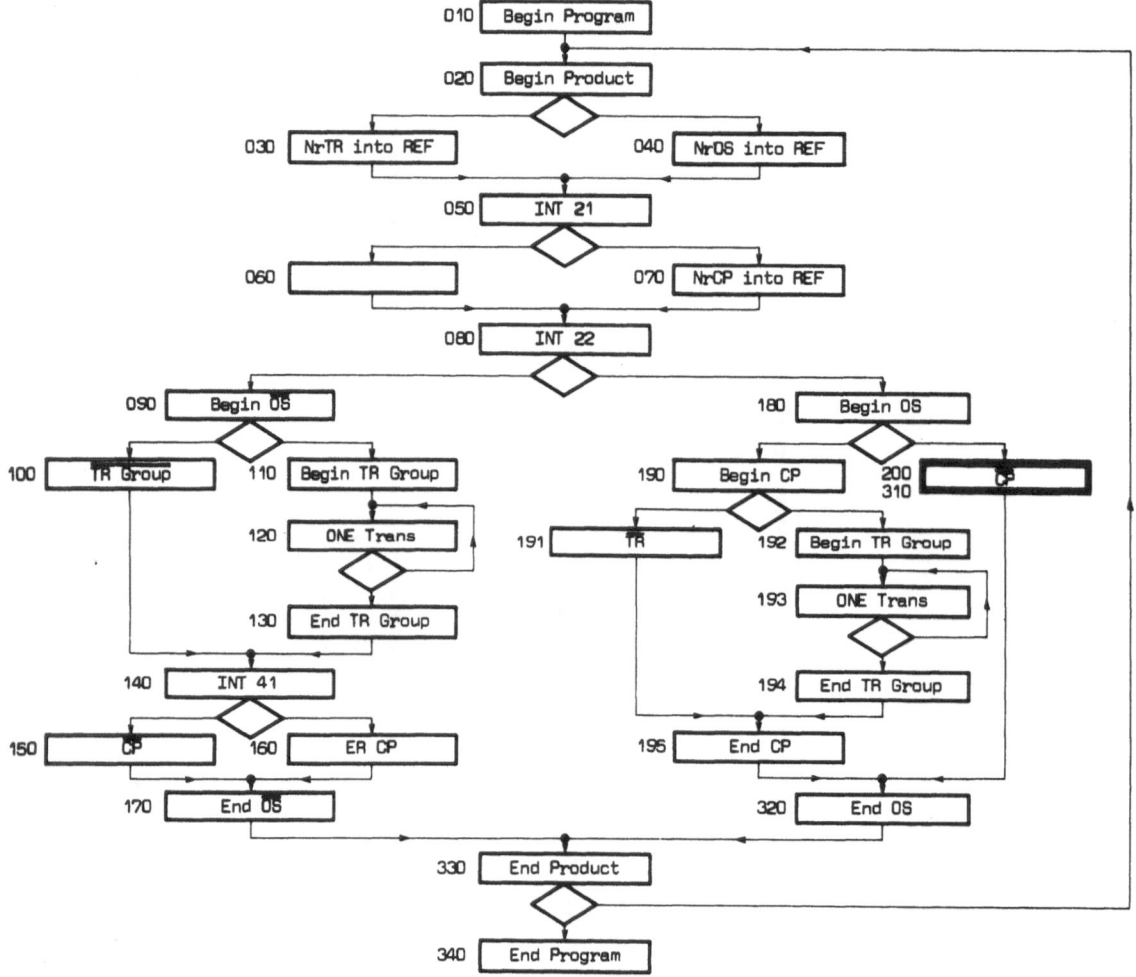

The symbol $\overline{CP}$ enclosed in a bold-lined box refers to the flowchart of logical sequences for the OS.CP subset of the program.

Flowchart of logical sequences for the subset of program which processes data for the condition OS.C̄P̄:

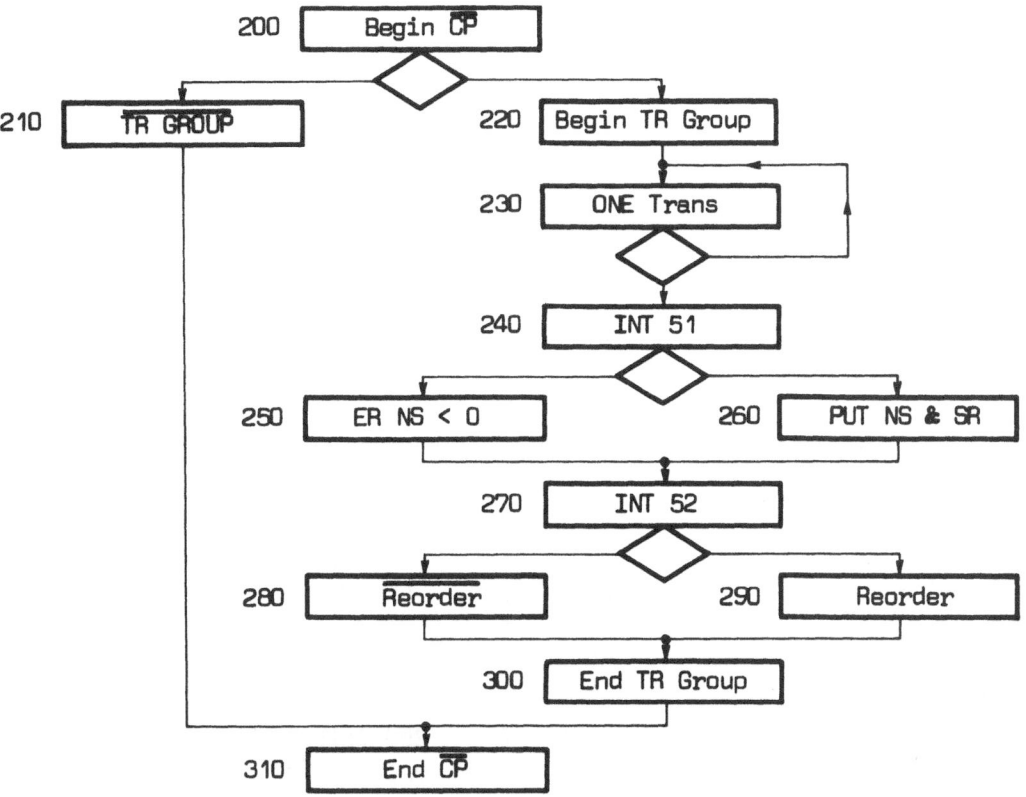

With the set Pl of logical program sequences redefined, it is time to redefine the set Pi. In practice, where changes are extensive, as is the case here, it is preferable to restructure entirely the detailed organization (set Pi). This is what we will do here, establishing:

- The list of instructions by category.
- The detailed and sequenced list of program instructions.

List of instructions by category:

010	GET 1st OS	
010	GET 1st TR	
010	GET 1st CP	
320	GET OS	
120	GET TR	
230	GET TR	
160	GET CP	
190	GET CP	
193	GET TR	
020	IF NrOS $<$ NrTR	040
030		050
050	IF NrCP $<$ NrREF	070
060		080
080	IF NrOS = NrREF	180
090	IF NrTR = NrREF	110
100		140
120	IF NrTR = NrREF	120
140	IF NrCP = NrREF	160
150		170
170		330
180	IF NrCP $\neq$ NrREF	200
190	IF NrTR = NrREF	192
191		195
193	IF NrTR = NrREF	193
195		320
200	IF NrTR = NrREF	220
210		310
230	IF NrTR = NrREF	230
240	IF QNS $\overline{< 0}$	260
250		270
270	IF QNS $<$ QMin-Stock	290
280		300
330	IF $\overline{EOF}$	020

040	NrOS into REF
030	NrTR into REF
070	NrCP into REF
220	ΣQTR = 0
230	ΣQTR + QTR
240	QNS = QOS + ΣQTR
290	QRO = QMax-Stock $-$ QNS
	S/R FMT NS Rec
290	FMT RO
250	QRO = 0
290	PUT RO
	S/R FMT SR NrREF. QOS, QNS
210	Spaces into ΣQTRSR
240	FMT ΣQTR
210	CALL S/R
260	CALL S/R
	S/R PUT SR & INIT
090	FMT NrER
250	FMT NrER
250	FMT QNS $<$ 0 MSG
090	FMT $\overline{OS}$ MSG
160	FMT $\overline{OS}$.CP.MSG
250	PUT ER & INIT
090	PUT ER & INIT
160	PUT ER & INIT
	S/R PUT NS

Detailed sequential list of program instructions

010	GET 1st OS	
	GET 1st TR	
	GET 1st CP	
020	IF NrOS < NrTR	040
030	NrTR into NrREF	050
040	NrOS into NrREF	
050	IF NrCP < NrREF	070
060		080
070	NrCP into NrREF	
080	IF NrOS = NrREF	180
090	FMT NrER	
	FMT $\overline{OS}$ MSG	
	PUT ER & INIT	
	IF NrTR = NrREF	120
100		140
110		
120	GET TR	
	IF NrTR = NrREF	120
130		
140	IF NrCP = NrREF	160
150		170
160	FMT CNCL MSG	
	GET CP	
	PUT ER & INIT	
170		330
180	IF NrCP ≠ NrREF	200
190	GET CP	
	IF NrTR = NrREF	192
191		195
192		
193	GET TR	
	IF NrTR = NrREF	193
194		
195		320
200	IF NrTR = NrREF	220
210	Spaces into ΣQTRSR	
	CALL S/R	310
220	ΣQTR = O	

230	ΣQTR + QTR	
	GET TR	
	IF NrTR = NrREF	230
240	QNS = QOS + ΣQTR	
	FMT ΣQTR	
	IF QNS $\overline{< 0}$	260
250	QRO = 0	
	FMT NrER	
	FMT QNS < 0 MSG	
	PUT ER & INIT	270
260	CALL S/R	
270	IF QNS < QMin-Stock	290
280		300
290	QRO = QMax-Stock − QNS	
	FMT RO	
	PUT RO	
300		
310		
320	GET OS	
330	IF $\overline{EOF}$	020
340		END
S/R	FMT NrSR, QOS, QNS	
	PUT SR & INIT	
	FMT NS Rec	
	PUT NS	

Third Example: modification of the set of output data, requiring the redefinition of the set of logical program sequences, PI.

Starting with the preceding program, we wish to add an output file, with a record for each product for which there is no OS record, but for which there is both a CP record and one or more TR records. We will call this the cancelled-products transactions file, CT.

New program diagram

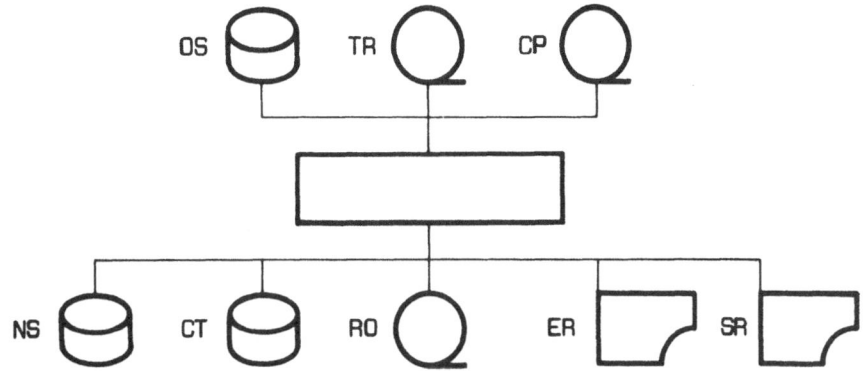

The file CT has 0 or I record for each product.

Product—Number (NrCT)	Transactions (ΣQTRCT)

Logical Output File

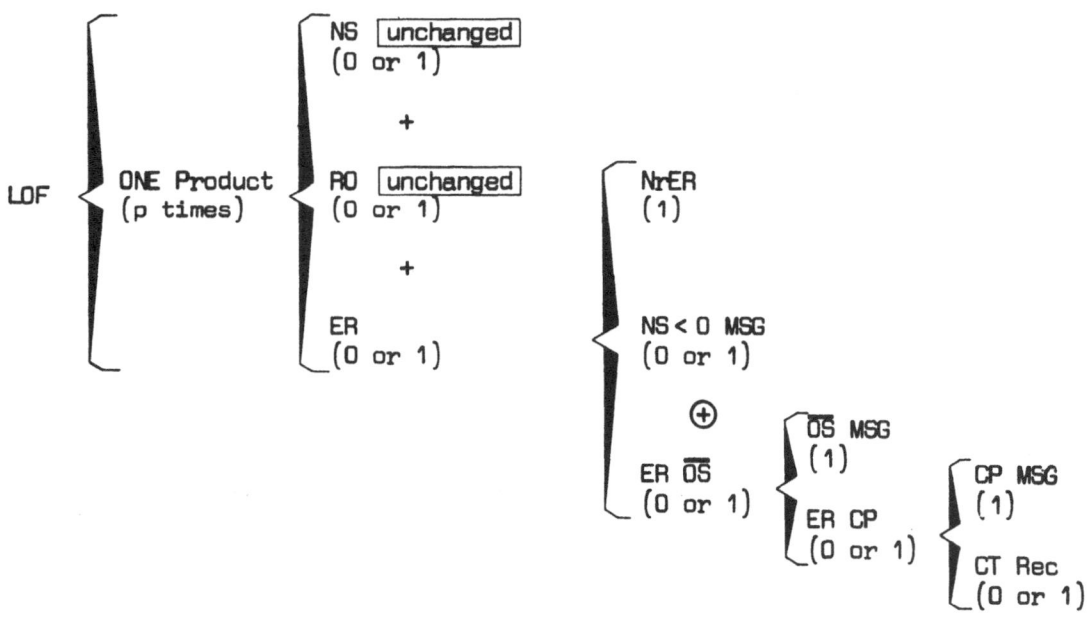

The process of writing the CT file has to be included in the product decision table.

ONE Product OS TR CP	ER $\overline{OS}$	OS into NS Spaces into ΣQTRSR PUT SR, NS	CALC ΣQTR, NS See T2	ER CP	CNCL	CT Rec
0 0 0	φ	φ	φ	φ	φ	φ
0 0 1	X			X		
0 1 0	X					
0 1 1	X			X		X
1 0 0		X				
1 0 1					X	
1 1 0			X			
1 1 1					X	

Inspection of the table shows that the subset $\overline{OS}$ should be modified

Program { ONE Product (p times) } { INT 22 (1) ; $\overline{OS}$ (0 or 1) } TR Group (0 or 1) } { Begin (1) ; ONE TR (t times) ; INT 41 (1) ; CP (0 or 1) ; $\overline{CP}$ (0 or 1) ; End (1) }

Flowchart of the set $\overline{OS}.TR$

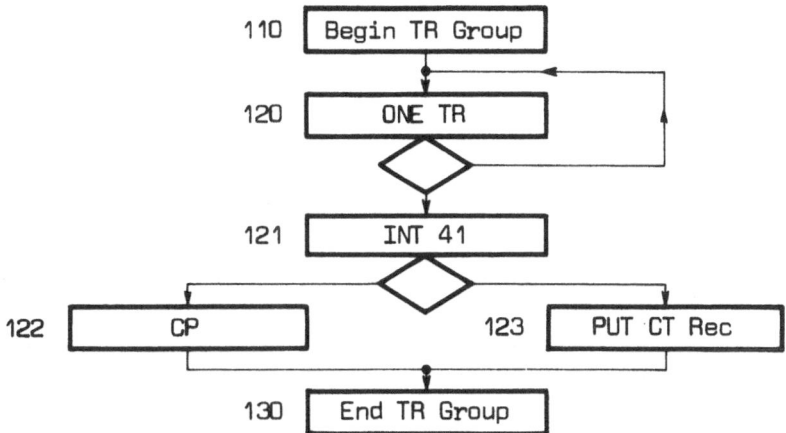

This last example shows how the tree-structured organization of sets allows the immediate identification of the place to be modified, in this case the subset TR Group at level 3 in the set ONE OS Product.

Having defined the set of logical sequences PI, it is time to redefine the set of instructions Pi, i.e. perform the detailed organization of the modified subset.

121	If NrCP = NrREF	123
122		130
110	ΣQTR = 0	
120	ΣQTR + QTR	
123	FMT CT Rec	
123	PUT CT	

Detailed and sequenced instruction list for the subset modified in the program:

110	ΣQTR = 0	
120	ΣQTR + QTR	
	GET TR	
	If NrTR = NrREF	120
121	If NrCP = NrREF	123
122		130
123	FMT CT Rec	
	PUT CT	
130		

Sequence 110, formerly empty, now contains an instruction. This sequence corresponds to the processing performed, at the start, on the set of transactions for a product with no old stock. Such data was not processed in the old version; after modification, the sum of transactions must be initialized at the indicated point.

We will now examine a case of program modification in which the set of logical sequences PI is modified: given a redefinition of the set of outputs, with inputs unchanged but differently used, it is necessary to modify the LIF since the criterion for the subdivision of input data is the number of times a subset is USED in the set. One can therefore state the following rule:

If physical input files are unchanged, but use of their data is modified, the LIF is modified and the set of logical sequences PI is redefined.

Take the preceding program in the form it has after the three modifications have been performed. It is now requested that the error report list replenishment transactions (i.e. $QTR < 0$) for products where there has been an error of the type $\overline{OS}$.

LOF redefinition

Here we show only the modified subsets, but recall that it is essential to keep program documentation perfectly up to date after every modification.

$$
\text{LOF} \left\{ \begin{array}{l} \text{ONE Product} \\ (p \text{ times}) \end{array} \right\} \left\{ \begin{array}{l} \text{ER} \\ (0 \text{ or } 1) \end{array} \right\} \left\{ \begin{array}{l} \text{ER } \overline{\text{OS}} \\ (0 \text{ or } 1) \end{array} \right\} \left\{ \begin{array}{l} \begin{array}{l} \text{OS MSG} \\ (1) \end{array} \\ \begin{array}{l} \text{RE Group} \\ (0 \text{ or } 1) \end{array} \left\{ \begin{array}{l} \text{ONE} \\ \text{Replenishment} \\ (r \text{ times}) \end{array} \right. \end{array} \right.
$$

RE = Replenishment (i.e. TR record with $QTR < 0$)

LIF redefinition

$$
\text{LIF} \left\{ \begin{array}{l} \text{ONE Product} \\ (p \text{ times}) \end{array} \right\} \left\{ \begin{array}{l} \text{TR Group} \\ (0 \text{ or } 1) \end{array} \right\} \left\{ \begin{array}{l} \text{ONE TR} \\ (t \text{ times}) \end{array} \right\} \left\{ \begin{array}{l} \begin{array}{l} \overline{QTR < 0} \\ (0 \text{ or } 1) \end{array} \\ \oplus \\ \begin{array}{l} QTR < 0 \\ (0 \text{ or } 1) \end{array} \end{array} \right.
$$

Modification takes place only in sequence 120.

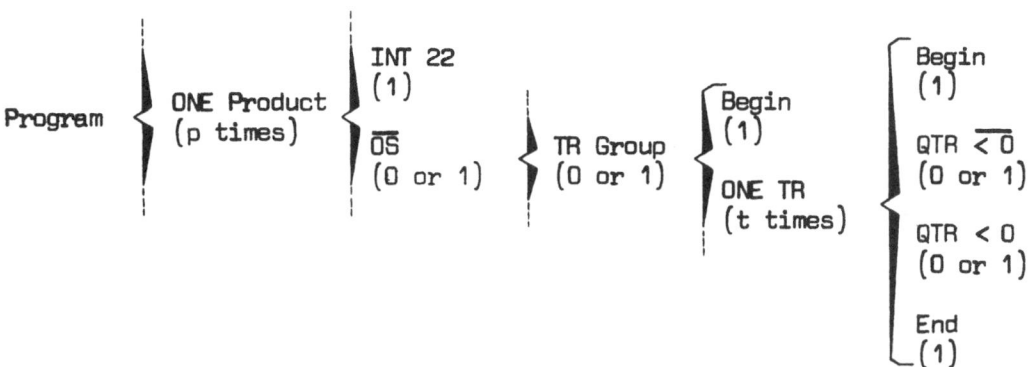

Flowchart

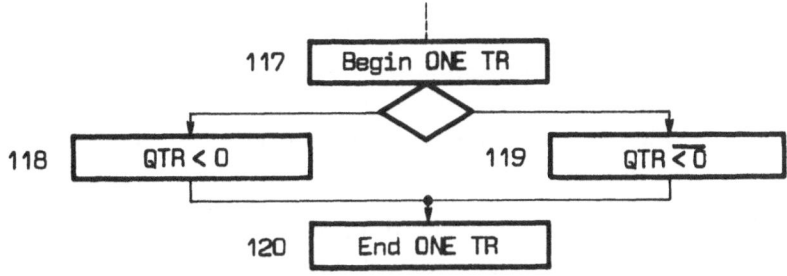

117	Begin ONE TR
118	QTR < 0
119	QTR $\overline{< 0}$
120	End ONE TR

Here is the detailed redefinition of the set of instructions Pi.

117	IF QTR $\overline{< 0}$	119
118		120
119	FMT OS.RE MSG	
119	PUT ER & INIT	

The detailed and ordered list for the modified sequences:

117	ΣQTR + QTR	
	If QTR $\overline{< 0}$	119
118		120
119	FMT OS.RE MSG	
	PUT ER & INIT	
120	GET TR	
	If NrTR = NrREF	117

To conclude this section on the modification of programs constructed on a hierarchical basis, we insist on this basic rule:

Any modification is performed by finding the subsets to be changed at the lowest level.

- **In the set of output data (LOF, LPF).**
- **In the set of input data (LIF, LPF).**
- **In the set P1 of the program.**

PROGRAM MAINTENANCE

When the record format of a physical file is to be altered, i.e. when fields are added, deleted, or changed in length, it is necessary to see what modifications will be required in all the programs that use the file. **Every data-processing service must consequently maintain a directory of files so that it is possible to identify immediately the list of programs that use them.** Establishing such a directory is much easier when the set of data in the system is organized in a tree structure, as described in our book 'Organisation des Données d'un Système'.

When the record format of a physical file is modified for one program, it is possible that the Logical Input Files for other programs using the file may be only slightly altered, or altered not at all. It is, however, always necessary to check the effect of changes on the location of data in memory, and particularly on the organization of file record fields.

CHECKOUT OF MODIFIED PROGRAMS

Program checkout takes place in three stages.
- Verification of the set of logical sequences PI, using the LOF.
- Verification of the set of program instructions Pi, also using the LOF.
- Verification on the computer: after compilation and correction of any syntax errors, the test consists in processing a set of test data to determine whether outputs are as expected.

We have already dealt with the first two checks.

- The first verifies that for each output item, and for the actions that prepare it, there exists the appropriate sequences.
- The second verifies that instructions intended to produce the output have in fact been programmed; and (although this may seem obvious) that what is not to be output is not in fact output.

Evidently, these two checks can be made only if the program and its data have been constructed as we recommend. They require very little extra effort, and permit a spectacular reduction in the number of test executions. Reducing the number of test executions has several consequences.

- A reduction in the programmer's work load for program corrections.
- An even greater reduction in the time taken to put programs into production.
- A reduction in machine-time requirements.

Some statistics are worth mentioning on this point. Several data-processing services have consented to give us the number of tests conducted on their systems during a one-year period, along with a count of the number of programs checked out during the year. Dividing the number of tests by the number of programs yields an average for tests-per-program. Since our study covers several thousand programs, we think that the results, however approximate, are of some interest.

- Services working with empirical methods have an average of 20 to 30 tests per program.
- Services using more or less the logical principles we recommend, without performing checks on logical sequences and instructions, report an average of 4 to 10 test executions per program.
- Services where programmers have thorough experience of hierarchical organization and perform thorough checks average fewer than two test executions per program.

We underline the fact that these last results derive from several dozen data-processing services in government, retailing, banking, manufacturing, and general service bureaus, located in a variety of countries.

In order to prevent the deterioration of a set of well-made programs, it is necessary to perform on modified programs checks just as rigorous as those performed on original programs. (Many so-called maintenance operations in fact deal with programming errors detected after the program was declared operational.) In both cases, it is indispensable to have test data which check out all logical sequences in the program.

Test data serve to produce models of reports and files corresponding to all requirements originally laid down for the program. Test data sets are defined as a function of the completed program; model reports and files are defined as a function of the Logical Output File. If the definition of outputs and of the set $\overline{OUTPUT}$ are checked and approved by the persons for whom the the program has been written, program outputs from execution using the test data set permit a complete check of program logic.

If output models are not determined on the basis of the Logical Output File and the set $\overline{OUTPUT}$, the test data set can only check that the completed program executes correctly.

Use of test data and output models provides a verification of the program output checks defined above.

Both for the initial test data set and for sets checking out subsequent modifications, the following rule applies:

A test data set checks all the logic of a program if and only if one can verify the surjection of the set of sequences tested by the data with the set of logical sequences PI.

In practical terms, for a test execution to check fully the logic of a program, it is necessary and it suffices that all possible paths in the program be verified at least once, i.e. each elementary structure must be tested twice.

- Two passages of an alternative structure, one per branch.
- Two passages of a repetitive structure R, one to verify that repetition takes place, and one to verify the exit from the loop.

Example: take the following program

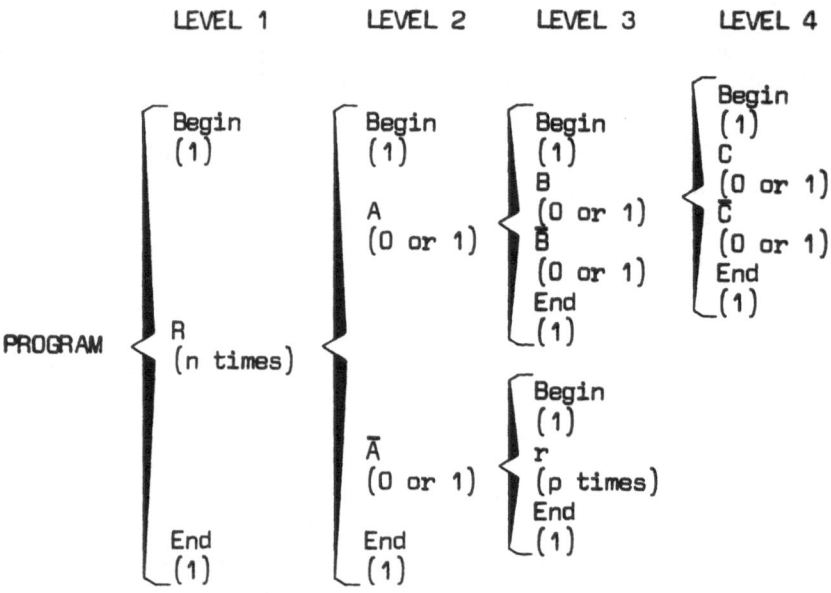

LEVEL 1   LEVEL 2   LEVEL 3   LEVEL 4

PROGRAM

Begin
(1)

R
(n times)

End
(1)

Begin
(1)

A
(0 or 1)

Ā
(0 or 1)

End
(1)

Begin
(1)
B
(0 or 1)
B
(0 or 1)
End
(1)

Begin
(1)
r
(p times)
End
(1)

Begin
(1)
C
(0 or 1)
C̄
(0 or 1)
End
(1)

Test data must perform these checks:

- At level 4, sequences C and $\overline{C}$ = 2 passages.
- At level 3, the subset B is already checked by execution of C and $\overline{C}$. It suffices to provide for execution of B, i.e. by one passage; plus the two passages through loop r,. which makes a total of three passages at level 3.
- At level 2, the subsets A and A are verified by the passages provided for the lower levels, as is the case for level 1.

Thus five passages through R are required to test all the sequences that make up the program.

Logical sequence flowchart

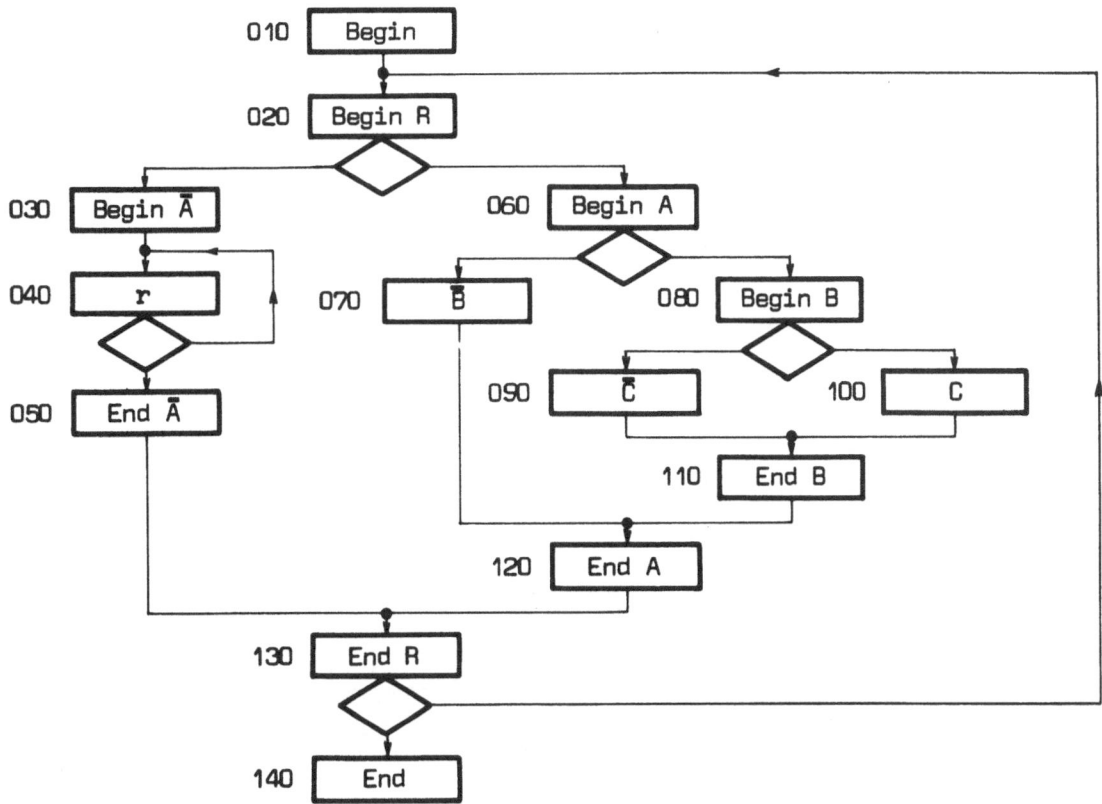

Execution of the test program

Passages through R:

1: 010, 020, 030, 040, 050, 130
2: 020, 030, 040, 040, 050, 130
3: 020, 060, 070, 120, 130
4: 020, 060, 080, 090, 110, 120, 130
5: 020, 060, 080, 100, 110, 120, 130, 140.

For the checkout of complex structures:

- Two passages suffice per loop to test a repetitive complex structure.
- Checkout of a complex alternative structure involves at most 2^n passages, where n is the number of simple alternatives making up the complex structure. It is possible to simplify test execution for complex alternative structures by eliminating impossible paths, as will be seen in the example that follows.

Take the original solution for the program presented at the beginning of this chapter, as shown in the following flowchart.

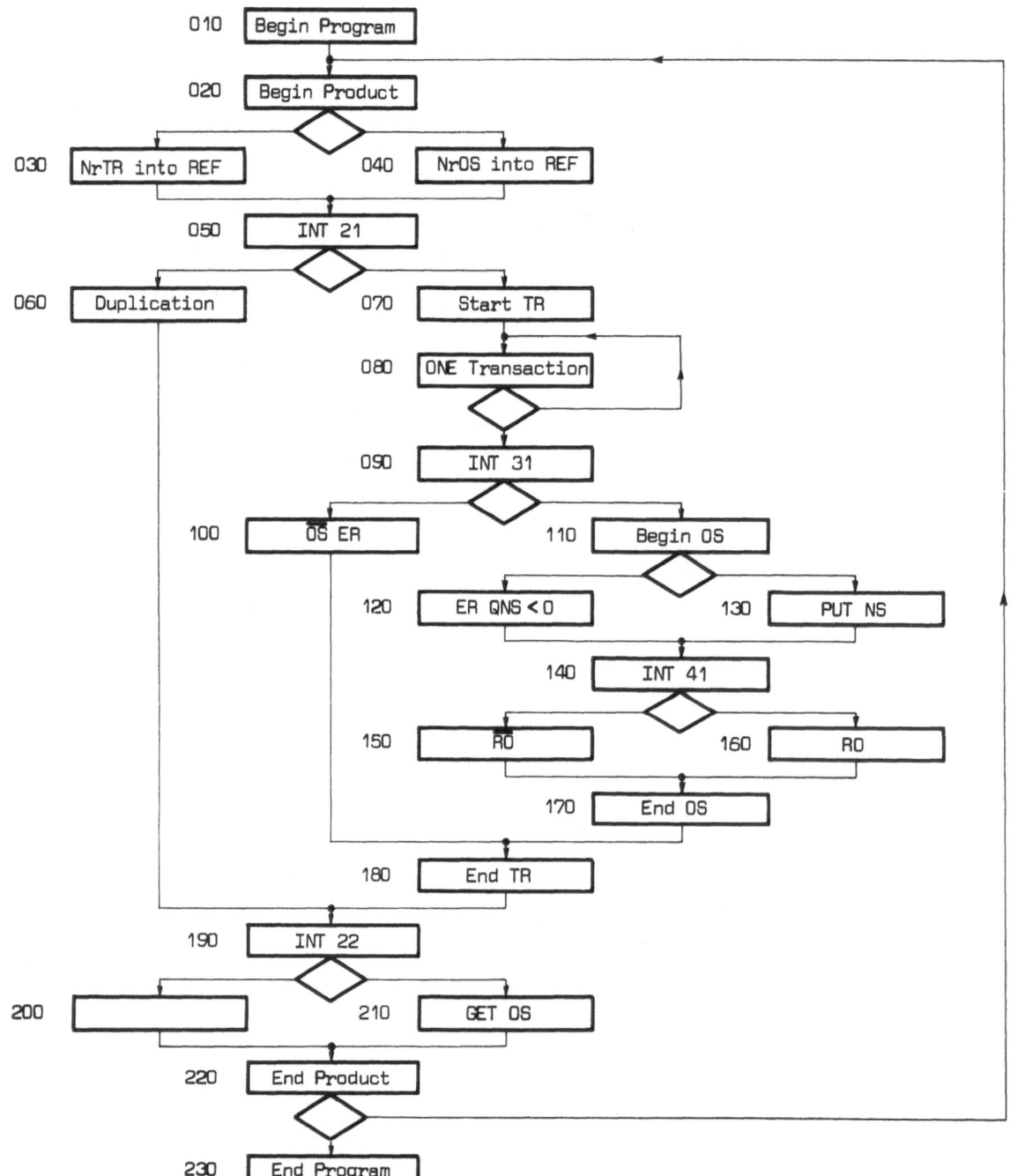

If we examine the complex alternative structure at level 4, sequences 110 to 170, we find that it is made up of two simple alternatives, thus $2^2 = 4$ passages. One is impossible: there can be no occurrence of a $QNS < 0$ error (sequence 120) followed by an RO process (sequence 150); three passages will suffice.

Now we can prepare the complete set of test data for the program.

- At level 4, there must be three passages.
- At level 3, a passage must be added to test sequence 100.
- At level 2, there must be $2^3 = 8$ passages. A truth table permits identification of impossible paths and of sequences already provided for.

LEVEL 2			Impossible	Covered
030	060	200		
0	0	0	X	
0	0	1	X	
0	1	0		
0	1	1	X	
1	0	0		X
1	0	1		X
1	1	0	X	
1	1	1	X	

'030, 060, 200' stand for execution of sequences 030, 060, and 200.

- 040, 070 is impossible since if NrOS < NrTR there is no transaction for the product.
- 040, 200 is impossible since if there is an old record, we pass on to 210 and read an OS record.
- 030, 060 is impossible since if we pass through 030, a group of transactions exists.
- 030, 070 is already tested by passages for lower levels.

Thus the total number of passages required (and sufficient) is five.

```
1:   010, 020, 040, 060, 190, 210, 220
2:   020, 030, 070, 080, 090, 100, 180, 190, 200, 220
3:   020, 030, 070, 080, 080, 090, 110, 130, 140, 160, 170, 180, 190, 210, 220
4:   020, 030, 070, 080, 090, 110, 120, 140, 160, 170, 180, 190, 210, 220
5:   020, 030, 070, 080, 090, 110, 130, 140, 150, 170, 180, 190, 210, 220, 230.
```

The number of records needed in the test files is as follows.

Passage	OS File	TR File
1	1	0
2	0	1
3	1	2
4	1	1
5	1	1

In total, four records plus the end-of-file mark for OS, and five records plus end-of-file for TR.

It remains to establish models for reports and output files. In our example there should be:

- Two lines in the error report, one for the $\overline{OS}$ error in the second passage, and one for the $QNS < 0$ error in the fourth passage.
- Three records in the NS file, produced by passages 1, 3, and 5.
- Two records in the RO file from passages 3 and 4.

Thus the Logical Output File for this example.

LEVEL 1   LEVEL 2

NS [dup / calc QNS $\overline{< 0}$]
(0 or 1)

+

LOF   ONE Product   RO [normal / error]
        (p times)   (0 or 1)

+

ER [$\overline{\overline{OS}}$ / QNS < 0]
(0 or 1)

A truth table allows determination of output models.

	Output NS	ONE Product Output RO	Output ER	Output NS DUP	Output QNS ≤0	RO Normal	RO Error	ER $\overline{OS}$	ER QNS < 0
0	0	0	0	○	○	○	○	○	○
1	0	0	1					X	
2	0	1	0	○	○	○	○	○	○
3	0	1	1				X		X
4	1	0	0	X	X				
5	1	0	1	○	○	○	○	○	○
6	1	1	0		X	X			
7	1	1	1	○	○	○	○	○	○

3 NS Records   2 RO Records   2 ER Records

The minterms 0 and 2 ($\overline{NS}.\overline{ER}$) as well as 5 and 7 (NS.ER) are empty by definition.

SUMMARY

Program development takes place in two stages.

- *Organization into logical sequences (set PI).*
- *Detailed organization and coding (set Pi).*

When modification has an effect on program logic, it is necessary to:

- *Modify the LOF.*
- *Modify the LIF.*
- *See whether the modification has an effect on processing phases other than the first; and if so, organize the data input to such phases.*
- *Check any truth tables present.*
- *Redefine the set PI.*
- *Redefine the set Pi and verify its mapping to set PI.*
- *Perform program checkout using outputs for the set PI, then for Pi, before final correction.*

Any modification of input files (LIF or LPF) requires modification of the set of program logical sequences, PI, and consequently that of the set of program instructions Pi. If the program derives from truth tables, and if the actions required for new outputs have an effect on data subsets, the set PI must likewise be modified.

If physical input files are unchanged, but use of the data they contain is modified, the LIF must be changed, and the set of logical sequences PI must be redefined.

Any program modification is performed by seeking the subsets to be modified at the lowest level:

- *In the set of output data (LOF, LPF).*
- *In the set of input data (LIF, LPF).*
- *In the program's PI set.*

After checking program output, a test data set permits checkout of the entire program if and only if it is possible to verify the surjection of the set of test data subsets to the set of program logical sequences PI.

3 — EVOLUTION OF EMPIRICAL AND STRUCTURED PROGRAMS

COMPLETE RESTRUCTURING OF EMPIRICAL PROGRAMS

Managers of computer services with well-trained personnel are strongly advised to profit from requests for modification of empirical programs by having them reconstructed and organizing their data into tree structures. In many cases the investment is less than one might expect, and exceedingly worthwhile when further modifications are requested.

In rewriting a program, the greatest difficulty is in the reconstruction of the statement of the problem. Where documentation is lacking, it is possible, with relative ease, to restate the problem by using the description of the physical input and output files processed.

Advantages of the hierarchical organization of programs appear fully only when all programs are so organized. The only problem that remains, having achieved this, is to bring new staff up to speed in logical programming techniques. Rapid turnover of programming staff can pose some problems, as can the use of temporaries and trainees.

EVOLUTION OF STRUCTURED PROGRAMS

The establishment of structured programming is certainly an improvement on empirical programming. We think, however, that the realization of entirely modifiable programs requires some attention to a few points that appear to have escaped previous notice.

- Input and output data, as well as program data, should be defined and treated as mathematical sets.
- Organization of data should take the form of successive subdivisions of sets.
- The logical organization of the program is deduced from that of the input data, itself derived from the output data and the processes which produce them.
- Program data must be carefully distinguished from the functions to which they give rise.

With these points in mind, let us examine the four elementary structures proposed by structured programming. We will see that they have some serious drawbacks for program modification; but that in contrast to empirical programs one can (taking into account the four points noted above) change such programs for easy subsequent modification.

First structure: the 'simple sequence'

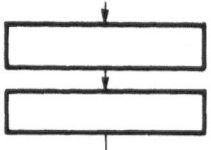

In terms of our definition of a logical sequence, the 'simple sequence' above, a chain of processes, amounts to one logical sequence, and only one. The fact that one is able to distinguish in such a chain the instruction subsets that correspond to different functions is important; but these subsets are more properly distinguished and ordered in the set of program instructions Pi. In contrast, in defining the set of logical sequences PI, a sequence forms an element which may not be represented by more than one symbol.

This is of some practical importance in view of the general tendency to descend too rapidly to details. The fact of having to define a set prevents any subdivision of an element until such time as it is to be redefined in its turn as a set. The principal defect of computer programs is that one too often organizes the set around the details rather than placing the details in the set.

Second structure: IF THEN ELSE

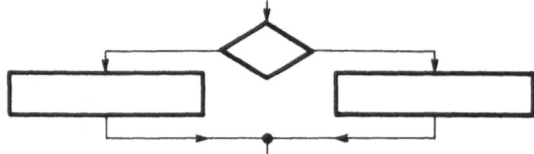

It is obvious how much this structure seems to resemble the alternative structure used in organizing a program hierarchically. But there is something missing: there are no beginning and ending sequences. This lack is a great inconvenience in program modification. Although in the initial solution such sequences may be empty, by definition the set of input data to which they correspond is not empty. Consequently, if modification causes instructions to appear in these sequences, they must be created, i.e. the set PI has to be redefined, which would have been needless had such sequences been evident in the first place.

It should be noted that the branch instruction symbolized in the flowchart corresponds to the existence of a beginning sequence which in an alternative structure can in no case be empty, since it contains by definition at least one branch. Moreover, to designate that this sequence contains only one instruction prejudices the detailed organization which, we believe, should not be attempted until all the logic of the program has been defined.

Third structure: DO UNTIL

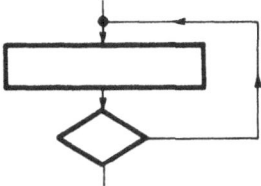

The remarks we would make concerning this structure are the same as those concerning the IF THEN ELSE structure. Let us add only that the separation of the branch symbol from the rectangle that precedes it shows that there is no notion of a logical sequence in structured programming: every branch instruction belongs in the same logical sequence as the data-processing and I/O operations that precede it.

Fourth structure: DO WHILE

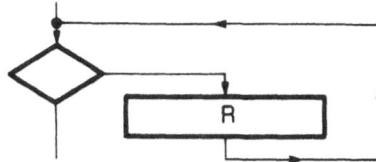

This fourth and final structure is not an elementary structure, but rather the nesting of a loop in an alternative structure. Since the sequence R is to be executed 0 to n times, it is more precisely a loop in one branch of an alternative. The DO WHILE structure is particularly ill-advised if it is desired eventually to modify the program.
Let us illustrate this last point with an example, taking a simplified stock-maintenance program.

Program diagram

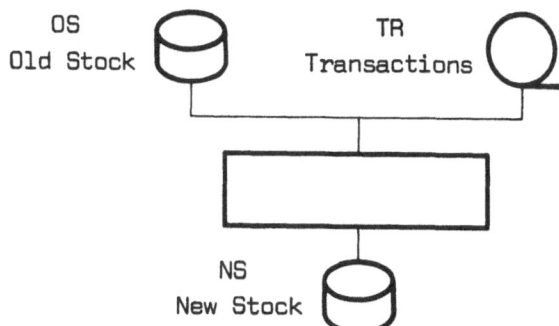

File NS, one record per product

Product—Number (NrNS)	Quantity (QNS)

File OS, one record per product (the case $\overline{OS}$.TR is excluded)

Product—Number (NrOS)	Quantity (QOS)

File TR, 0 to n records per product

Product—Number (NrTR)	Quantity +/− (QTR)

All files are sorted in ascending product-number order

Flowchart (a DO WHILE structure enclosed in a DO UNTIL)

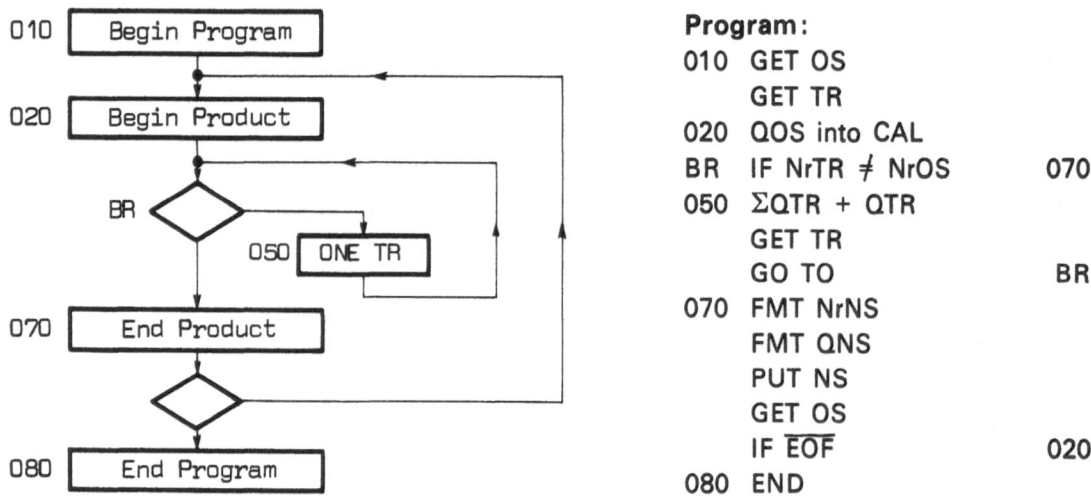

Program:

```
010  GET OS
     GET TR
020  QOS into CAL
BR   IF NrTR ≠ NrOS            070
050  ΣQTR + QTR
     GET TR
     GO TO                     BR
070  FMT NrNS
     FMT QNS
     PUT NS
     GET OS
     IF EOF                    020
080  END
```

The problem is to effect the following modifications:

• Print a list of products for which no transaction occurred, file TC.
• Produce a file of all products for which one or more transactions did occur, file TP.

File TC, 0 or 1 record per product

Product—Number (NrTP)	Transactions (ΣQTR)

File TP, 0 or 1 record per product

Product—Number (NrTC)

Whatever solution chosen requires modification of program logic. Here is one possibility.

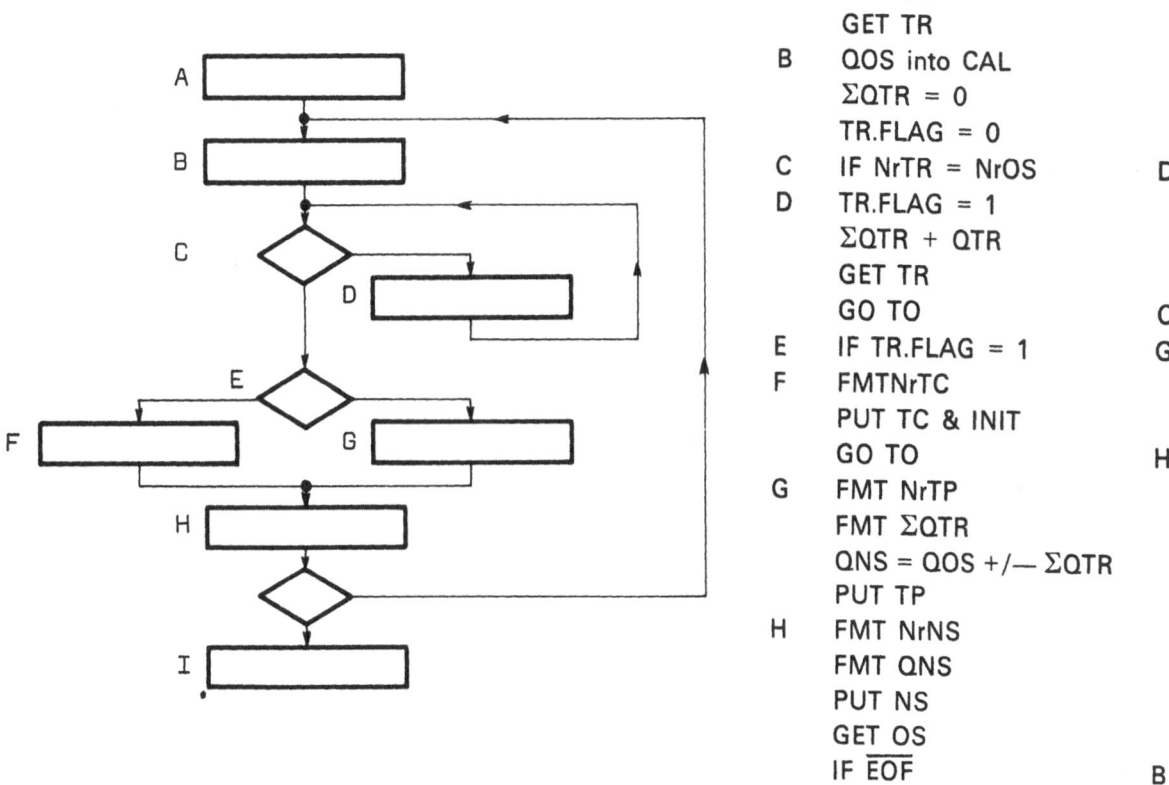

```
A    GET OS
     GET TR
B    QOS into CAL
     ΣQTR = 0
     TR.FLAG = 0
C    IF NrTR = NrOS              D
D    TR.FLAG = 1
     ΣQTR + QTR
     GET TR
     GO TO                      C
E    IF TR.FLAG = 1             G
F    FMTNrTC
     PUT TC & INIT
     GO TO                      H
G    FMT NrTP
     FMT ΣQTR
     QNS = QOS +/— ΣQTR
     PUT TP
H    FMT NrNS
     FMT QNS
     PUT NS
     GET OS
     IF EOF                     B
I    END
```

Now we will see how a hierarchical organization would have allowed us to deal with the problem, by comparing elements of the original and the modified program.

- Organization of the LOF and the LIF.
- Organization of the program as an ordered set of logical sequences, set Pl.
- Detailed organization, set Pi.

Logical Output File

$$\text{LOF} \left\{ \begin{array}{l} \text{ONE Product} \\ \text{(p times)} \end{array} \right\} \left\{ \begin{array}{l} \text{NrNS} \\ \text{(1)} \\ \vdots \\ \text{QNS [DUP/CALC]} \\ \text{(1)} \end{array} \right.$$

Logical Input File

$$\text{LIF} \left\{ \begin{array}{l} \text{ONE Product} \\ \text{(p times)} \end{array} \right\} \left\{ \begin{array}{l} \text{TR Group} \\ \text{(0 or 1)} \end{array} \right\} \left\{ \begin{array}{l} \text{ONE TR} \\ \text{(t times)} \end{array} \right.$$

Program

$$\text{PROGRAM} \left\{ \begin{array}{l} \text{Begin} \\ \text{(1)} \\ \\ \text{ONE Product} \\ \text{(p times)} \\ \\ \text{End} \\ \text{(1)} \end{array} \right. \left\{ \begin{array}{l} \text{Begin} \\ \text{(1)} \\ \\ \text{TR Group} \\ \text{(0 or 1)} \\ \\ \overline{\text{TR Group}} \\ \text{(0 or 1)} \\ \\ \text{End} \\ \text{(1)} \end{array} \right\} \left\{ \begin{array}{l} \text{Begin} \\ \text{(1)} \\ \\ \text{ONE TR} \\ \text{(t times)} \\ \\ \text{End} \\ \text{(1)} \end{array} \right.$$

Sequence flowchart

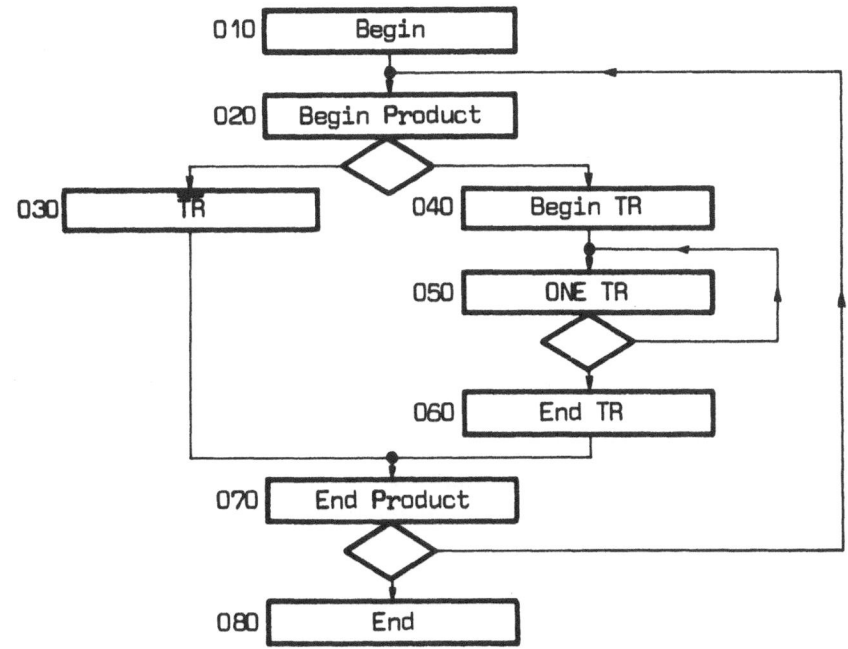

Set Pi

010	GET OS	
010	GET TR	
070	GET OS	
050	GET TR	
020	If NrTR = NrOS	040
030		070
050	If NrTR = NrOS	050
070	If $\overline{EOF}$	020
020	QOS into CAL	
050	ΣQTR + QTR	
070	FMT NrNS	
070	FMT QNS	
070	PUT NS	

Detailed and ordered list of instructions

010	GET OS		060	
	GET TR		070	FMT NrNS
020	QOS into CAL			FMT QNS
	If NrTR = NrOS	040		PUT NS
030	GO TO	070		GET OS
040				If $\overline{EOF}$ 020
050	ΣQTR + QTR		080	End
	GET TR			
	If NrTR = NrOS	050		

If we compare the two solutions prior to modification, we find that the tree-structured one, which we recommend, has one more conditional branch than the structured-programming solution. We will see the usefulness of this additional branch in the modified program.

Modified solution

The Logical Input File is unchanged; and, since there are no decision tables, the logical organization of the program is also unchanged. In other words, the set of logical sequences, PI, has not been redefined. Only the instruction set Pi has to be altered, as we shall see. Note that checking set PI against the LOF permits us to confirm that logical organization remains unaltered.

The same **flowchart of logical sequences** remains valid.

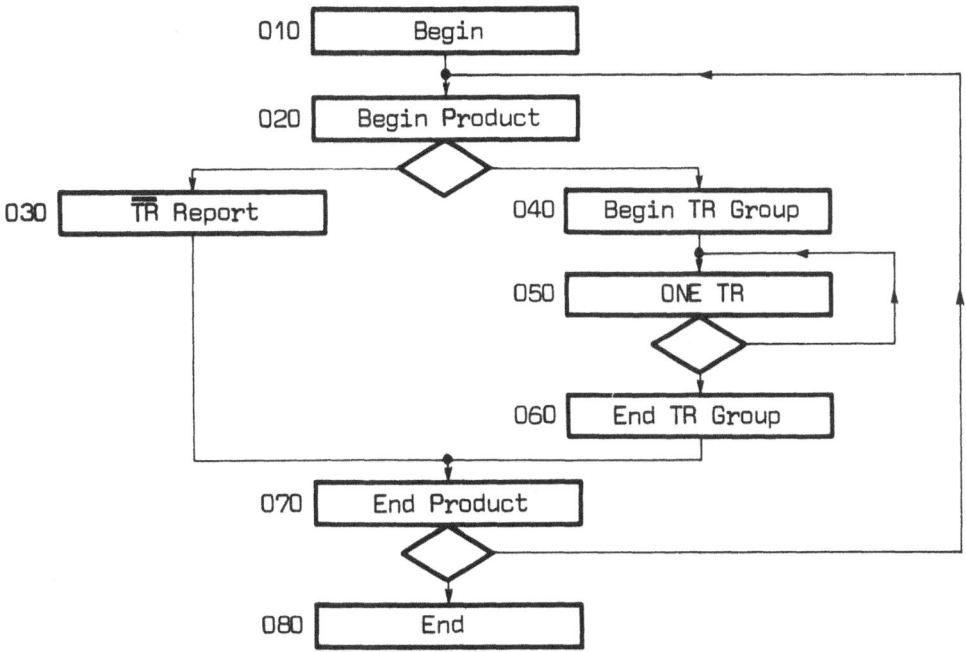

New instructions in the **detailed organization.**

040 ΣQTR = 0	060 PUT TP
060 QNS = QOS +/— ΣQTR	
060 FMT NrTP	030 FMT NrTC
060 FMT ΣQTR	030 PUT TC & INIT

Detailed and ordered list of instructions

010	GET OS		060	QNS = QOS +/— ΣQTR	
	GET TR			FMT NrTP	
020	QOS into CAL			FMT ΣQTR	
	IF NrTR = NrOS	040		PUT TP	
030	FMT NrTC		070	FMT NrNS	
	PUT TC & INIT	070		FMT QNS	
040	ΣQTR = 0			PUT NS	
050	ΣQTR + QTR			GET OS	
	GET TR			IF $\overline{EOF}$	020
	IF NrTR = NrOS	050	080		End

Let us now compare the two solutions.

The instructions added in the solution we prefer are seven in number, and all serve to perform calculations or outputs. In the solution derived from structured programming it was necessary to add eleven instructions, seven as in our solution, plus four others to handle the logic:

- One initialization of a flag.
- One setting of the flag.
- One conditional branch.
- One unconditional GO TO.

The deficit of our original solution was that it contained an extra conditional branch. Now the situation is reversed, since the modified structured-programming solution has a superfluous initialization of a flag, setting of the flag, and a GO TO. Moreover this latter solution executes the INIT QTR even where there are no transactions for a product, and sets the flag for every transaction. We believe, however, that these defects are minor compared to the difficulty of checking the organization of a structured program in the absence of a Logical Output File.

In practical terms, we advise that whenever a DO WHILE structure is encountered in a program, it should be replaced by the loop contained in an alternative structure.

In general, when modifying structured programs:

- If sufficient resources are available, i.e. enough time and well-trained personnel, programs should be constructed so as to have logical input and output files (and any logical phase files required) from which a hierarchical structure for each program may be derived.
- If only minor program modifications are required, subsets of 'simple sequences' should be grouped together into logical sequences; and the beginning and ending sequences should be added for alternative and repetitive structures. In short, an exact definition of the set PI should be constructed.

To sum up, it has to be taken into account that data constitute mathematical sets to be organized hierarchically; and that the set PI must be clearly distinguished from set Pi. When these basic principles are accepted and implemented, the result is programs easily modified, yielding good performance, and thoroughly documented.

4 — CONCLUSION

Before going on to the second part of this book, made up of exercises and suggested solutions, we would like to draw the reader's attention to the major points we have sought to illustrate in the preceding pages.

- The programmer who is given the task of modifying and developing existing programs should not be considered, nor should he consider himself, as some sort of 'second-class citizen'.
- In the current state of affairs, it is difficult for him to be considered otherwise, since the maintenance of empirical programs, and even of modular or structured programs, is irritating work, difficult to manage.
- It seems to us that constructing programs on a hierarchical basis is the only way in which programs can be made responsive to the evolving needs of their users. The distinction between set PI and set Pi is fundamental, as is the possibility of cross-checking between them.

Finally, we would like to say a word or two to educators in order to underline the importance, both theoretical and practical, of the subject matter presented in this book.

- The future programmer-analyst should design programs with a view to their evolution. In no way does this mean he should somehow foresee the modifications that will be requested; but rather he should correctly define the data, and then the sets PI and Pi.
- The future programmer-analyst must learn to modify existing programs, for this part of his work is not something he can make up as he goes along.

Before going any further, consider this question: in the examinations and tests given in training centers, schools, and universities, how many problems do we find that have to do with the evolution of programs and the data they process?

Part 2

PRACTICE

1 — REPORTS AND INPUT CHECKS

INTRODUCTION

The problems and exercises that follow are designed to progress from one to the next; they should be resolved in the sequence given. At each step in the series there is a solution to allow the reader to correct any mistakes he may have made. This should permit everyone to work through to the end of this section. It may happen that you will find a correct solution which differs from the one we propose. We suggest that you adopt our solution in working the exercises that follow so as to make it easier to understand their solutions.

The commentary on each solution is intended to reinforce the reader's theoretical and practical understanding, and should be read with close attention.

We will examine successively four programs and their modification. We will thus encounter some of the problems most frequently found in applications programming, in particular:

- Report Writing.
- Input Checking.
- Statistics.
- File Updating.
- Payroll Processing.

Our objective is to permit the reader to train himself to resolve logical problems found in all programs, well beyond the limits of the types covered here. For that reason you will find calculations in a report-writing problem, report-writing in a payroll problem, etc.

Finally, we have not sought to make the problems especially difficult, but rather to illustrate the fundamental rules of the design and transformation of programs, based on the elementary rules given in the book 'Conception des Données d'un Système'.

PROBLEM: PRINTING INVOICES

Program flowchart

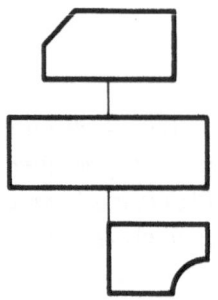

For input, there is a card file, TR.

The output is a collection of invoices, gathered in a file we will call IV. Each invoice consists of one or several pages. No customer is to receive more than one invoice.

A single-page invoice has the following format.

PREPRINTED AREA		
Customer–Number (CNr)	Customer–Name (CN)	Place-of-Delivery (PD)
Order–Number (ONr)	Address (ADR)	Date–Shipped (DS)
Customer's–Reference (CRF)	City–State–ZIP (CSZ)	Shipment–Number (SNr)

Product–Number (PNr)	Product–Name (PN)	Quantity (Q)	Unit–Price (UP)	Total–Price (TP)	Sales–Tax (TX)
				Totals (Σ T)	Sales–Tax (Σ TX)

Invoice–Date (IVD)	Payment–Method (PM)	%–Discount (%D)	Discount (D)	Net–Total (N Σ T)

Some products are tax-exempt; where no product is subject to the sales tax, no TX entry is to appear. Similarly, where there is no discount, the fields % D and D are to be blank.

A multi-page invoice begins with a page in the following format.

```
┌─────────────────────────────────────────────────────────────────────────────┐
│                                                                               │
│                       P R E P R I N T E D   A R E A                           │
│                                                                               │
│  ┌─────────────────────────────┬──────────────────────┬─────────────────────┐│
│    Customer-Number               Customer-Name          Place-of-Delivery    │
│       (CNr)                         (CN)                    (PD)              │
│    Order-Number                    Address               Date-Shipped        │
│       (ONr)                         (ADR)                   (DS)              │
│    Customer's-Reference          City-State-ZIP          Shipment-Number      │
│       (CRF)                         (CSZ)                   (SNr)             │
│                                                                               │
│  Product-Number  Product-Name   Quantity  Unit-Price  Total-Price  Sales-Tax │
│     (PNr)           (PN)           (Q)       (UP)        (TP)        (TX)     │
│  _____   _____    _____  _____  _____  _____  │
│  _____   _____    _____  _____  _____  _____  │
│  _____   _____    _____  _____  _____  _____  │
│                                                                               │
│                                                        Totals      Sales-Tax │
│                                                        (Σ T)       (Σ TX)    │
└─────────────────────────────────────────────────────────────────────────────┘
```

The values ΣT and ΣTX (if present) are partial totals accumulated since the beginning of the current invoice. They are reprinted at the head of the following page. If $\Sigma TX = 0$, the corresponding fields are to be blank.

Any other invoice page;

```
┌──────────────────────────────────────────────────────────────────────────┐
│                                                                            │
│                       P R E P R I N T E D   A R E A                        │
│                                                                            │
├──────────────────────────────────────────────────────────────────────────┤
│   Page—Number                                      Totals      Sales—Tax   │
│     (PG)                                          (Σ T)       (Σ TX)       │
│                                                                            │
│                                                                            │
│                                                                            │
│                                                                            │
├──────────────────────────────────────────────────────────────────────────┤
│                                                    Totals      Sales—Tax   │
│                                                   (Σ T)       (Σ TX)       │
│                                                                            │
│   Invoice—Date   Payment—Method   %—Discount  Discount  Net—Total         │
│     (IDV)          (PM)            (%D)        (D)      (N Σ T)            │
│                                                                            │
└──────────────────────────────────────────────────────────────────────────┘
```

After the preprinted area, which contains the company's letterhead, pages other than the first begin with the page number and, on the same line, a repeat of the totals found at the bottom of the preceding page. The skip to head-of-form is to be made after the fourth product line of a page (i.e. after the 10th line of the page; we will call the line counter LCT).

Now the physical input file. Each invoice derives from:

- One customer-card (1 per invoice).
- One order-card (1 per invoice).
- One shipment-card (1 per invoice).
- n product-cards (p per invoice).

	CC	Customer-Number (CNr)	Customer-Name (CN)	Address (ADR)	City-State-ZIP (CSZ)	
Customer-Card	1	Customer-Number (CNr)	Customer-Name (CN)	Address (ADR)	City-State-ZIP (CSZ)	
Order-Card	CC 2	Customer-Number (CNr)	Order-Number (ONr)	Customer's-Ref (CRF)	%-Discount (%D)	Payment-Method (PM)
Shipment-Card	CC 3	Customer-Number (CNr)	Shipment-Number (SNr)	Place-of-Delivery (PD)	Shipment-Date (SD)	
Product-Card	CC 4	Customer-Number (CNr)	Product-Number (PNr)	Product-Name (PN)	Quantity (Q) · Unit-Price (UP) · %-Sales-Tax (%TX)	

Card sequence has not been checked.

Calculations

- Per product: $TP = Q \times UP$
  ADD TP to ΣT

  If $\%TX < 0$: $TX = \dfrac{TP \times \%TX}{100}$

  ADD TX to ΣTX.

  If LCT = 10, perform the transition to a new page; we will call this process PAGE.

- Per invoice: If $\Sigma TX = 0$, blank the ΣTX field.

  If $\%D > 0$, $D = \dfrac{\Sigma T \times \%D}{100}$

  $N\,T = \Sigma T - D + \Sigma TX$

  If $\overline{\%D < 0}$, N T $= \Sigma T + \Sigma TX$.

Now let us set up the Logical Output File (LOF). Special care must be taken in establishing the LOF where printer files are present.

Logical Output File

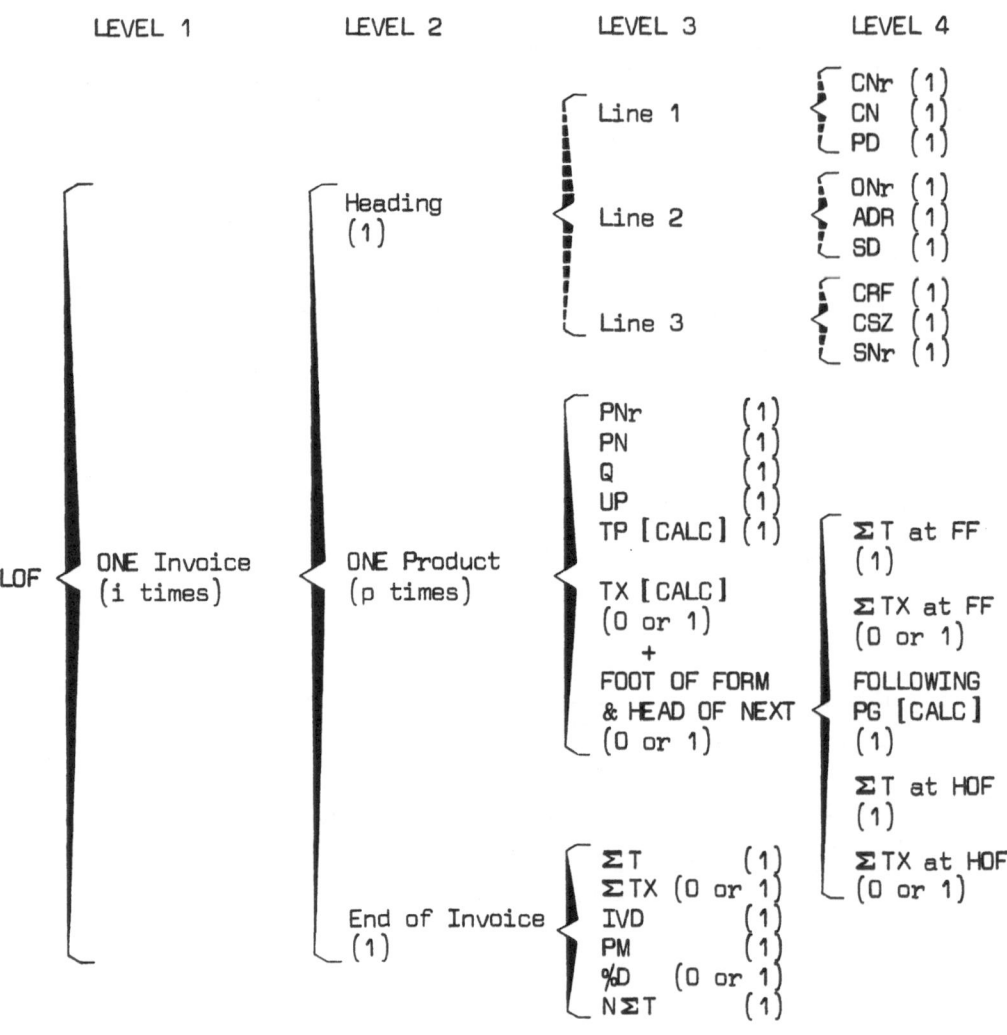

$\overline{\text{OUTPUT}} = \varphi$

Now construct the Logical Input File (LIF) and then any Logical Phase Files (LPFs) that may be required. Check your results against ours before continuing with the problem.

Logical Input File

$$\text{LIF} \left\{ \begin{array}{l} \text{ONE Invoice} \\ (\text{i times}) \end{array} \left\{ \begin{array}{l} \text{ONE Product--Card} \\ (\text{p times}) \\ \\ \%D[>0:\ 0/1] \end{array} \right. \right.$$

Logical Phase File

A **second processing phase** is required, since we cannot know in advance which invoices will have TX = 0.

$$\text{LPF2} \left\{ \text{ONE Invoice} \left\{ \Sigma\,TX\,[>0:\ 0/1] \right. \right.$$

There is a **third phase** at the product level, since we do not know after which product-line in the report we will have to change pages. We will use the mnemonic PAGE as an abbreviation for this process.

$$\text{LPF3} \left\{ \text{ONE Product} \left\{ \text{LCT } [=10:\ 0/1] \left\{ \Sigma\,TX\,[>0:\ 0/1] \right. \right. \right.$$

Now perform the subdivision of the program and draw up its flowchart.

Solution for the **tree structure of the program**

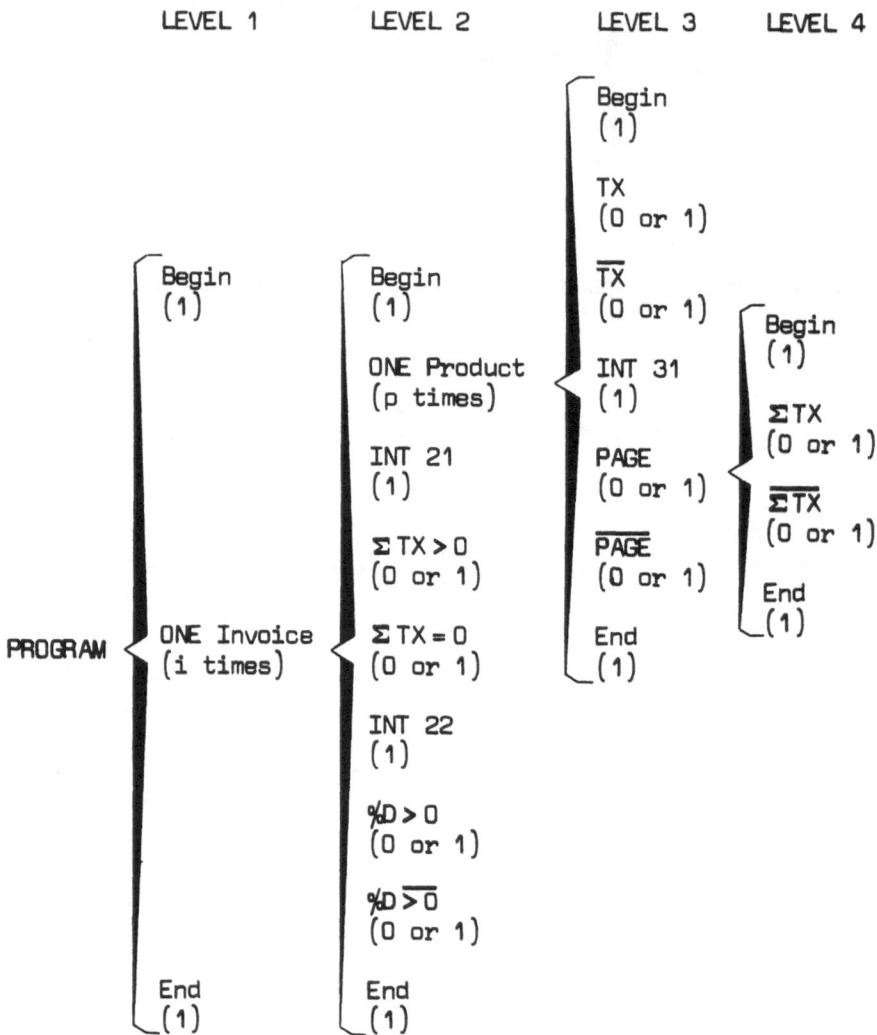

Solution for the **logical sequences flowchart**

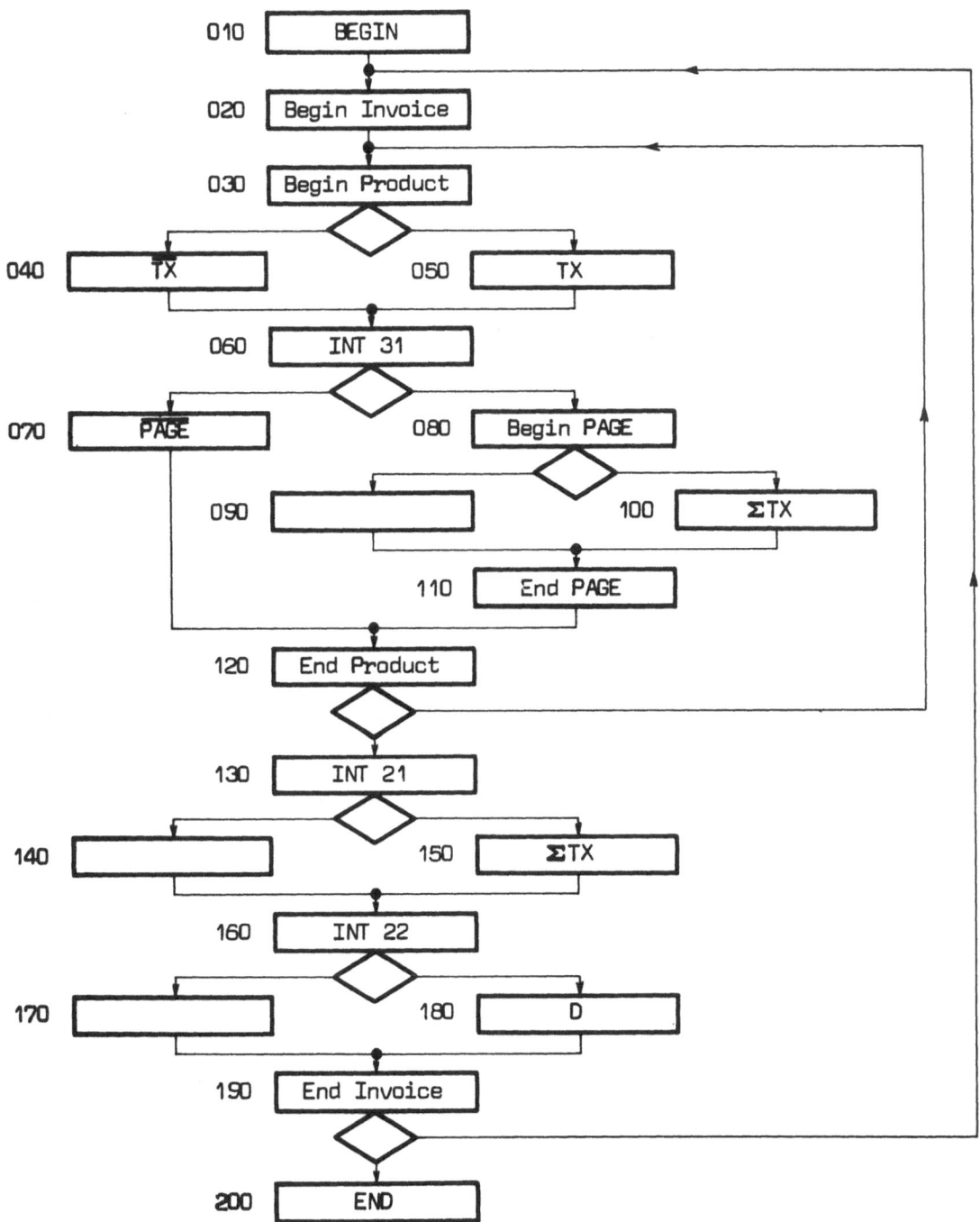

Check your solution using the LOF. See that the number of elementary structures in the flowchart is in fact equal to the number of elementary structures in the tree-structure diagram.

Now you can proceed to the detailed organization of the program, and define the set of instructions Pi. Check your solution against the LOF; see that the number of conditional branches is equal to the number of elementary structures, and the number of unconditional branches equal to the number of alternative structures; then compare your solution to that given opposite before going on to make the sequenced instruction list.

List of instructions by category

010 GET 1st TR		
020 GET TR		
020 GET TR		
020 GET TR		
120 GET TR		
030 IF %TX > 0	050	
040	060	
060 IF LCT = 10	080	
070	120	
080 IF ΣTX > 0	100	
090	110	
120 IF CNr = REFNr	030	
130 IF ΣTX > 0	150	
140	160	
160 IF %D > 0	180	
170	190	
190 IF $\overline{\text{EOF}}$	020	

020 INIT LCT
030 LCT + 1
020 CNr into REF
110 INIT LCT
030 TP = Q × UP X
030 ΣT + TP

$$050 \quad TX = \frac{TP \times \%TX}{100}$$

050 ΣTX + TX
020 INIT ΣT
020 INIT ΣTX

$$180 \quad D = \frac{\Sigma T \times \%D}{100}$$

150 N ΣT = ΣT + ΣTX
180 N ΣT = N ΣT — D
020 INIT PG
080 PG + 1

020 FMT CN-Line
020 ADR into WRK
020 CSZ into WRK
020 Order-Card into WRK
020 FMT PD
020 PUT 1st Line & INIT
020 FMT ADR-Line
020 PUT 2nd Line & INIT
020 FMT CSZ-Line
020 PUT 3rd Line & INIT
030 FMT Product-Line
050 FMT TX
060 PUT Product-Line & INIT
080 FMT ΣT
100 FMT ΣTX
110 PUT Foot-Line & INIT
110 FMT PG
110 PUT Head-Line & INIT
130 FMT ΣT
150 FMT ΣTX
160 PUT ΣT-Line & INIT
160 FMT IVD
160 FMT PM
180 FMT %D & D
190 FMT N ΣT
190 PUT N ΣT-Line & INIT

Watch out for work-area data, which may be overwritten before you are through with them: Order-Card and Customer-Card.

Sequenced list of program instructions

010	GET 1st TR	070	120
020	INIT PG	080	FMT ΣT
	INIT LCT		PG + 1
	CNr into REF		IF ΣTX > 0	100
	FMT CN-Line	090		110
	ADR into WRK	100	FMT ΣTX
	CSZ into WRK	110	PUT Foot-Line & INIT
	GET Order-Card TR		FMT PG
	Order-Card into WRK		PUT Head-Line & INIT
	GET Shipment-Card TR		INIT LCT
	FMT PD	120	GET TR
	PUT 1st Line & INIT		IF CNr = REFNr	030
	FMT ADR-Line	130	FMT ΣT
	PUT 2nd Line & INIT		N ΣT = ΣT
	FMT CSZ-Line		IF ΣTX > 0	150
	PUT 3rd Line & INIT	140		160
	INIT ΣT	150	N ΣT = ΣT + ΣTX
	INIT ΣTX		FMT ΣTX
	GET Product-Card TR	160	PUT ΣT-Line & INIT
030	LCT + 1		FMT IVD
	TP = Q × UP		FMT PM
	ΣT + TP		IF %D > 0	180
	FMT Product-Line	170		190
	IF %TX > 0	050		

$$\text{180} \quad D = \frac{\Sigma T \times \%D}{100}$$

040		060	
050	$TX = \dfrac{TP \times \%TX}{100}$		N ΣT = N ΣT — D
	ΣTX + TX		FMT %D
	FMT TX		FMT D
060	PUT Product-Line & INIT	190	FMT N ΣT
	IF LCT = 10	080	PUT N ΣT-Line & INIT
			IF $\overline{\text{EOF}}$	020
200			END

MODIFICATION PROBLEM

We should make clear that this really is a problem, and not a simple course exercise. The solution demands some thought and a strict adherence to the logical principles we have described earlier.

Let us suppose that the solution to the preceding problem, implemented on an old card-processing computer, did not give satisfactory results because the cards were frequently out of sequence. Now it is requested that the program check for all possible sequence errors.

* Wherever such errors occur in the header-cards, the corresponding invoice is not to be printed.
* When an error is detected, no further cards with that customer-number are to be processed.
* A card file ER is to be produced, giving (for any such error in the header- or product-cards) the customer-number being processed at the time of the error, and the customer-number and card-code of the card found to be out of sequence.

Error record (ER) format.

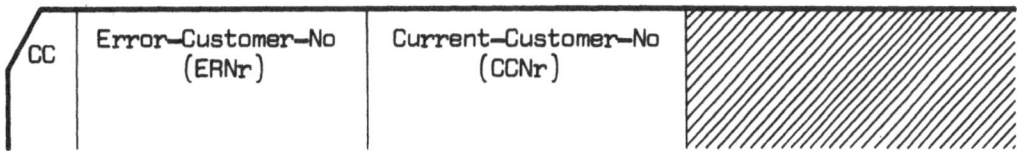

* At the 10th error, the program is terminated by forcing the end-of-file condition. The error count is maintained in a field, ECT.

Error conditions

* If the first card for a customer has CC ≠ 1.
* If the cards read on the second, third, or fourth GET have:
    * CNr ≠ REFNr
    * CC ≠ (preceding CC + 1)
* If following cards for the same customer have CC ≠ 4.

Checking of the three header-cards for an invoice takes place before beginning the processing and printing of the invoice; which therefore requires storage of their contents in a work area during the check.

Modify the LOF, LIF, and LPFs.

Modified Logical Output File

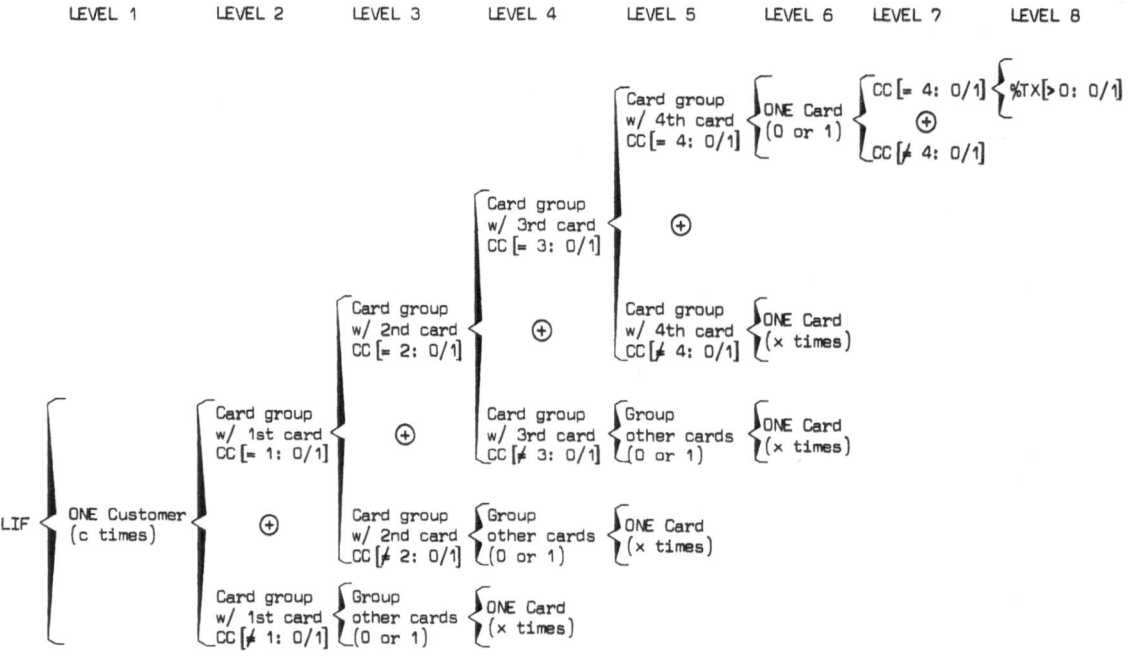

LOF { ONE Customer (c times) } { ONE Invoice unchanged (0 or 1) (Except for end-of-invoice (0 or 1) + ONE ER-Card (0 or 1) } { CC ERNr CCNr (1) } [Missing card, duplicate card, misplaced card, erroneous CC, erroneous customer-no]

Modified Logical Input File

LEVEL 1   LEVEL 2   LEVEL 3   LEVEL 4   LEVEL 5   LEVEL 6   LEVEL 7   LEVEL 8

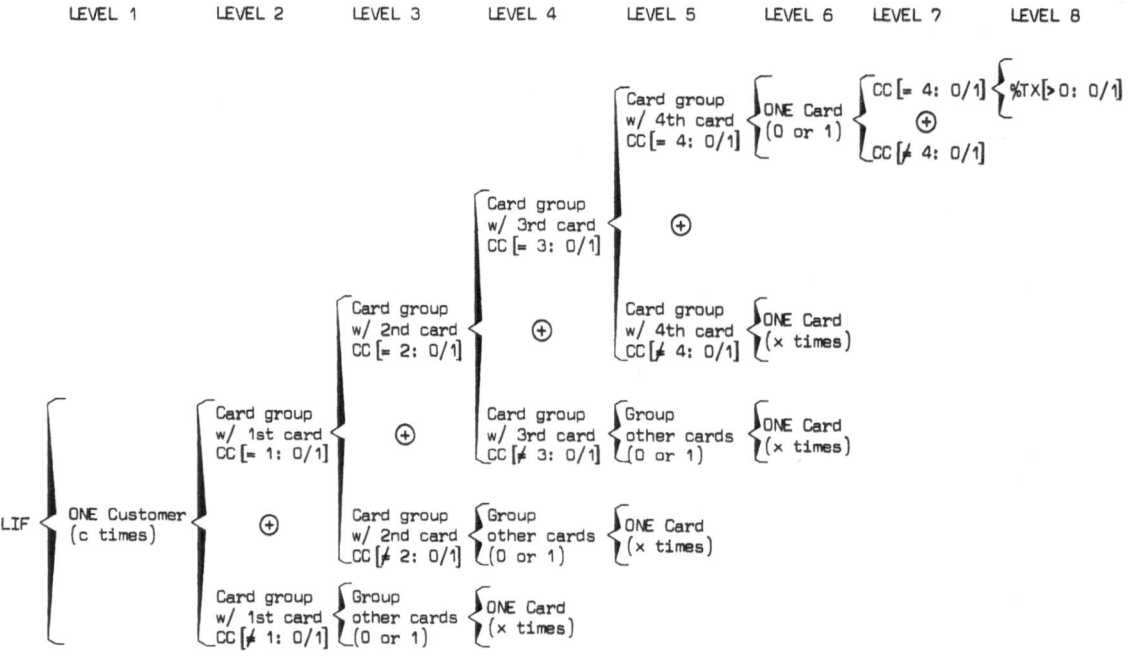

Logical Phase Files

$$\text{LPF2} \left\{ \text{ONE Customer} \left\{ \begin{array}{l} \text{ER } [= 1: 0/1] \\ \text{ER } [= 0: 0/1] \left\{ \%\text{D } [>0: 0/1] \right. \end{array} \right. \right.$$

$$\text{LPF3} \left\{ \begin{array}{l} \text{ONE Customer} \\ \text{ER } = 1 \end{array} \right. \left\{ \text{ECT } [= 10: 0/1] \right.$$

$$\text{LPF4} \left\{ \begin{array}{l} \text{ONE Customer} \\ \text{ER } = 0 \end{array} \right. \left\{ \Sigma \text{TX } [>0: 0/1] \right.$$

$$\text{LPF5} \left\{ \text{ONE Product} \left\{ \text{LCT } [= 10: 0/1] \left\{ \Sigma \text{TX } [= 0: 0/1] \right. \right. \right.$$

$$\text{LPF6} \left\{ \text{CC} \ne 4 \text{ in 4th Card} \left\{ \text{1ER } [= 1: 0/1] \right. \right.$$

Here ER is a flag which indicates whether the file ER is to be produced; and 1ER, a flag indicating whether the current error is the first one.

Tree structure for the modified program

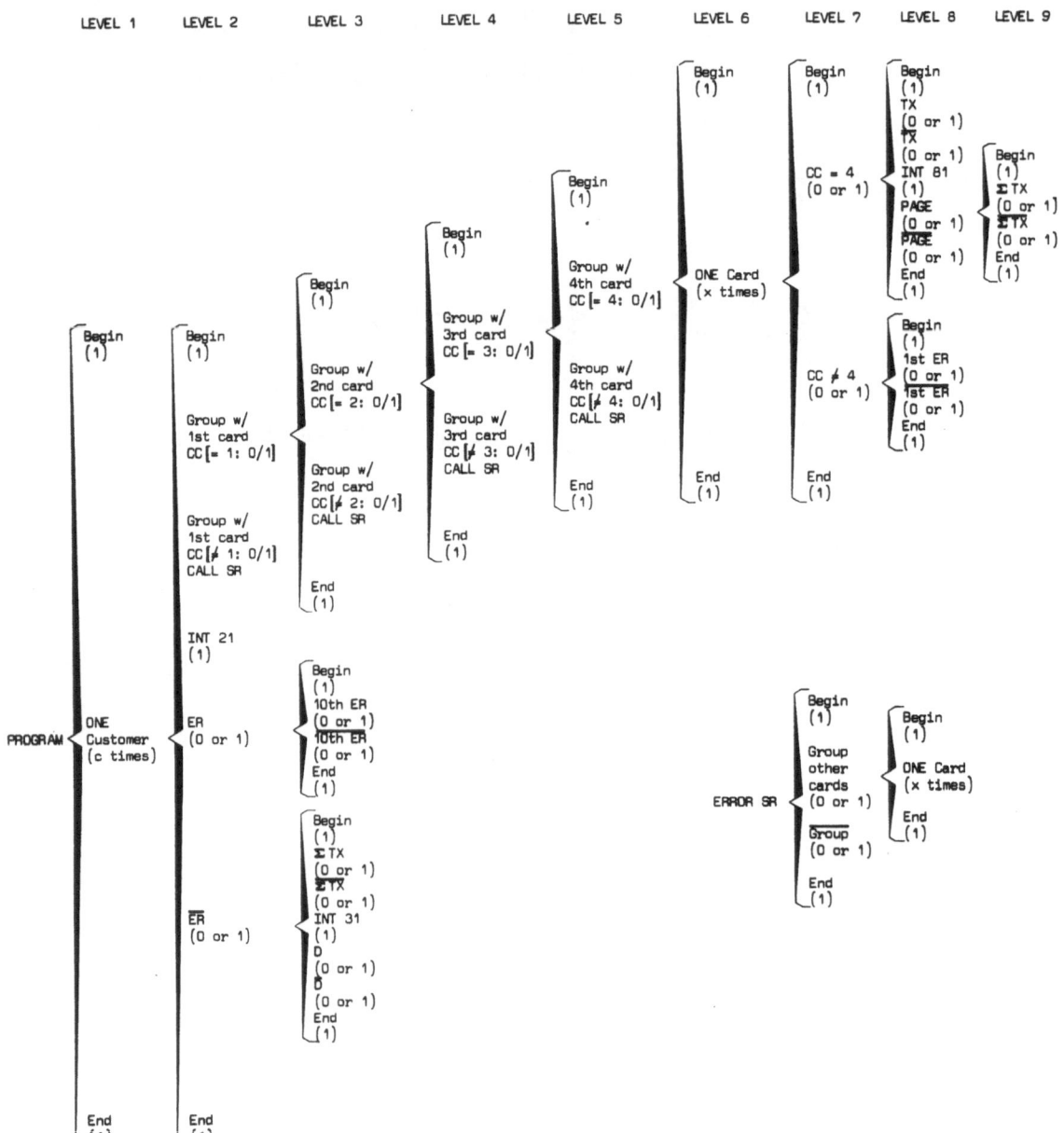

Flowchart for the first six levels

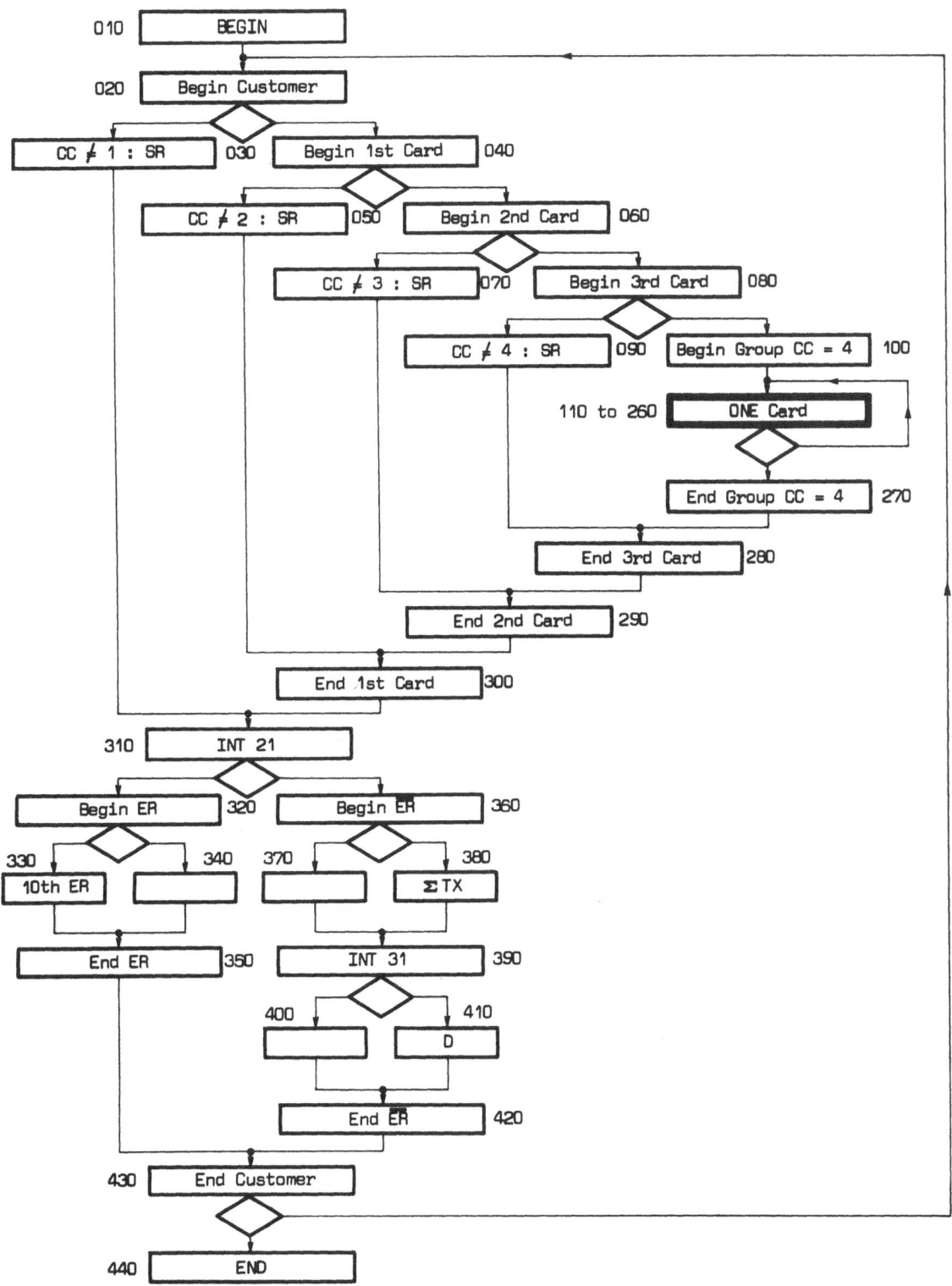

Flowchart for the set ONE Card

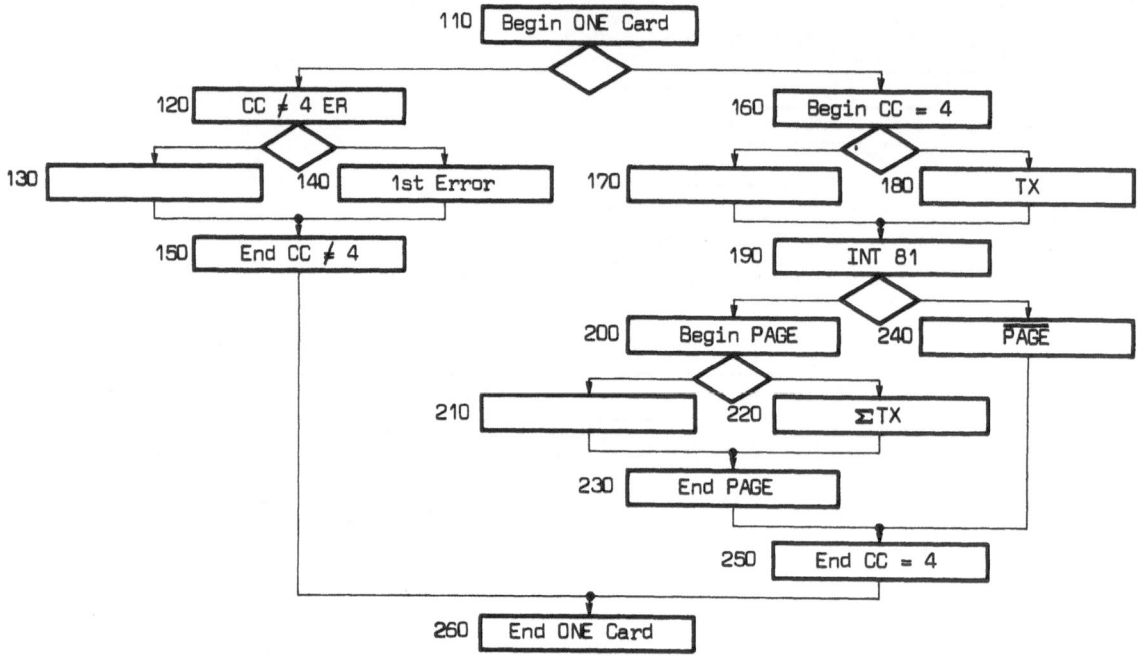

Flowchart for the error subroutine

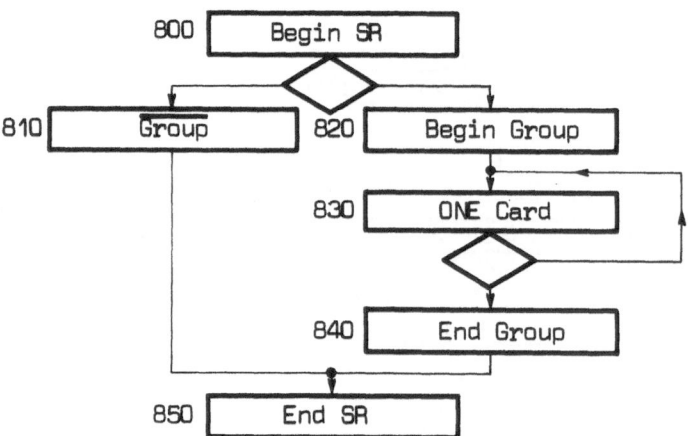

Because the modifications made are extensive, the list of instructions by category and the sequenced list have to be entirely redone. Do them now.

Note that for any fairly complex problem, there exist several ways of arriving at a solution which is both correct and constructed on a logical basis. If your solution does not correspond with the one we suggest here, check it out carefully; and then examine closely our solution so that you fully understand what we have done.

List of instructions by category

010 GET 1st TR		
040 GET TR		
060 GET TR		
080 GET TR		
260 GET TR		
830 GET TR		
020 IF CC = 1	040	
030	310	
040 IF CC = 2. CNr = REFNr	060	
050	300	
060 IF CC = 3. CNr = REFNr	080	
070	290	
080 IF CC = 4. CNr = REFNr	100	
090	280	
110 IF CC = 4	160	
120 IF 1 ER = 0	140	
130	150	
150	260	
160 IF % TX > 0	180	
170	190	
190 IF LCT < 10	240	
200 IF ΣTX > 0	220	
210	230	
230	250	
260 IF CNr = REFNr	110	
310 IF ER = 0	360	

320 IF ECT < 10	340
330	350
350	430
360 IF ΣTX = 0	380
370	390
380 N ΣT = ΣT + ΣTX	
390 IF % D > 0	410
400	420
430 IF $\overline{\overline{EOF}}$	020
800 IF CNr = REFNr	820
810	850
830 IF CNr = REFNr	830

100 1 ER = 0
140 1 ER = 1
020 CNr into REF
020 INIT LCT
230 INIT LCT
160 LCT + 1
010 ER = 0
350 ER = 0
800 ER = 1
150 ER = 1
010 INIT ECT
320 ECT + 1
160 TP = Q × UP
160 ΣT + TP

$$180 \quad TX = \frac{TP \times \%TX}{100}$$

180 ΣTX + TX

$$410 \quad D = \frac{\Sigma T \times \%D}{100}$$

410 N ΣT = N ΣT — D

800 FMT CC ER Card
800 FMT ERNr
800 FMT CCNr
140 FMT ER Card
340 PUT ER
040 Card 1 into WRK
060 Card 2 into WRK
080 Card 3 into WRK
100 FMT CN-Line
100 PUT INV & INIT
100 FMT ADR-Line
100 PUT INV & INIT
100 FMT CSZ-Line
100 PUT INV & INIT
180 FMT TX
190 FMT Product-Line

190 PUT INV & INIT
220 FMT ΣTX
230 FMT ΣT
230 PUT INV
230 FMT PG
230 PUT INV & INIT
020 INIT PG
200 PG + 1
330 Force EOF
360 FMT ΣT
380 FMT ΣTX
390 PUT INV & INIT
410 FMT D
420 FMT Net-Line
420 PUT INV & INIT

030 CALL ER SR
050 CALL ER SR
070 CALL ER SR
090 CALL ER SR

Sequenced instruction list

010	ER = 0		190	FMT Product-Line	
	INIT ECT			PUT INV & INIT	
	GET 1st TR			IF LCT < 10	240
020	CNr into REF		200	PG + 1	
	INIT LCT, PG			IF ΣTX > 0	220
	IF CC = 1	040	210		230
030	CALL ER SR	310	220	FMT ΣTX	
040	Card 1 into WRK		230	INIT LCT	
	GET TR			FMT ΣT	
	IF CC = 2. CNr = REFNr	060		PUT INV	
050	CALL ER SR	300		FMT PG	
060	Card 2 into WRK			PUT INV & INIT	250
	GET TR		240		
	IF CC = 3. CNr = REFNr	080	250		
070	CALL ER SR	290	260	GET TR	
080	Card 3 into WRK			IF CNr = REFNr	110
	GET TR		270		
	IF CC = 4. CNr = REFNr	100	280		
090	CALL ER SR	280	290		
100	FMT CN-Line		300		
	PUT INV & INIT		310	IF ER = 0	360
	FMT ADR-Line		320	ECT + 1	
	PUT INV & INIT			IF ECT < 10	340
	FMT CSZ-Line		330	Force EOF	350
	PUT INV & INIT		340	PUT ER	
	1 ER = 0		350	ER = 0	430
110	IF CC = 4	160	360	FMT ΣT	
120	IF 1 ER = 0	140		IF ΣTX > 0	380
130		150	370		390
140	FMT ER Card		380	FMT ΣTX	
	1 ER = 1			N ΣT = ΣT + ΣTX	
150	ER = 1	260	390	PUT INV & INIT	
160	LCT + 1			IF %D > 0	410
	TP = Q $\times$ UP		400		420
	ΣT + TP				
	IF %TX > 0	180	410	$D = \dfrac{\Sigma T \times \% D}{100}$	
170		190			
180	$TX = \dfrac{TP \times \%TX}{100}$			N ΣT = N ΣT — D	
				FMT D	
	ΣTX + TX		420	FMT Net-Line	
	FMT TX			PUT INV & INIT	
			430	IF $\overline{\text{EOF}}$	020
			440		END

The error subroutine

800	ER = 1		810		850
	FMT CC ER Card		820		
	FMT ERNr		830	GET TR	
	FMT CCNr			IF CNr = REFNr	830
	IF CNr = REFNr	820	840		
			850	End SR	

This exercise is an example of the nearly total reconstruction of a program. The rules given in the first part of this book should make it possible, when a modification is requested, to estimate the amount of work involved and the time it will take to do it. In this way a realistic schedule can be established, one which creates a normal working environment for the programmers while providing a satisfactory service to the computer's end users.

2 — STATISTICS

PROBLEM

A publisher wishes to have an annual statistical report on the sales and returns for each of his customers, retail bookstores. The report is to contain one line for each title sold or returned by a given bookstore.

Program diagram

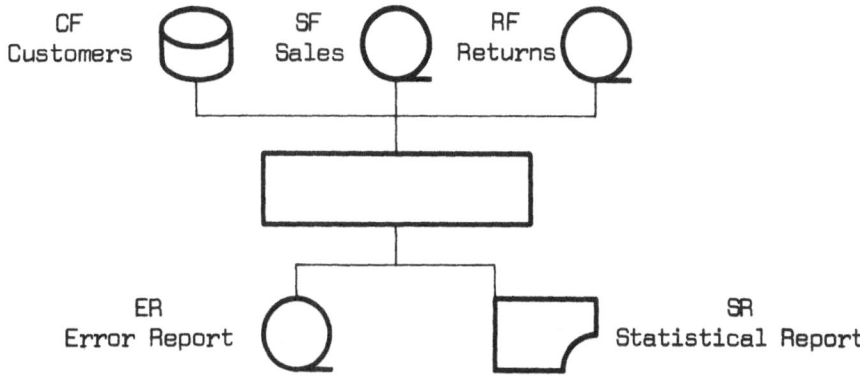

Outputs

Statistical-Report (SR) format

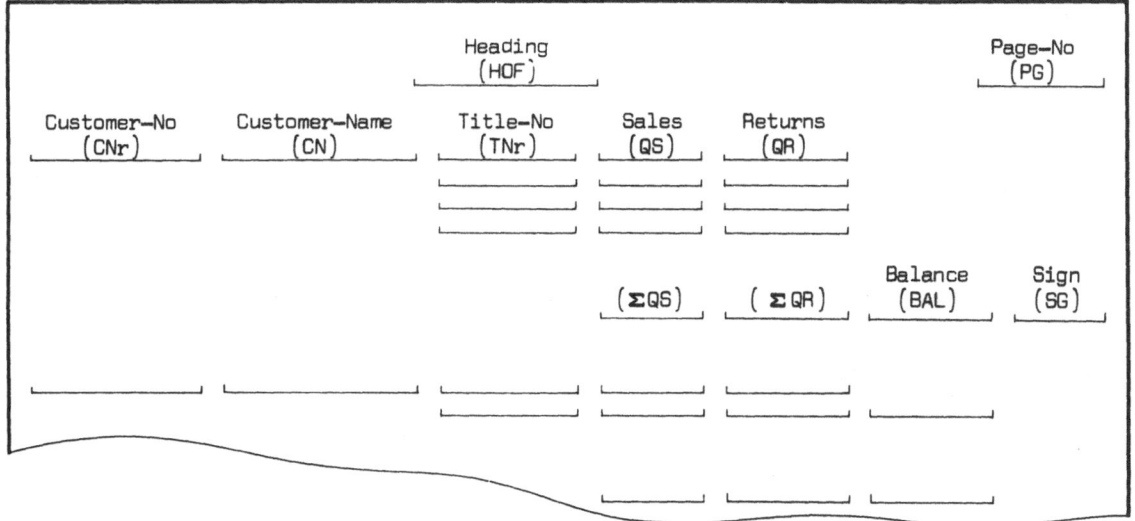

Sales (QS) and Returns (QR) are expressed as the number of copies per title sold or returned during the year; the Balance (BAL) gives the net dollar value of the year's transactions with the customer bookstore. Sign (SG) indicates whether the Balance is due or owed; DB where the customer owes the publisher; CR where the value of returns exceeds that of sales. Where the Balance is zero, the word ZERO appears in Sign (SG).

For any given title, there may be sales, returns, or both. For any given customer there may be no sales, or no returns; if there are neither, the customer has no entry in the report.

Error-Report (ER) format

Customer–No (ECNr)

An ER record is to be produced for each customer figuring in SF or RF for whom no record exists in CF.

Inputs

Customers file (CF), 0 or 1 record per bookstore, ordered on ascending customer-number (CCNr) and processed sequentially.

Customer–No (CCNr)	Customer–Name (CN)	Address (ADR)	Balance (CBAL)

Sales file (SF), 0 to n records for each title sold to a given customer, ordered on customer-number (SCNr) and title-no (STNr).

Customer–No (SCNr)	Title–No (STNr)	Quantity (SQ)	Total–Sales (TS)

Returns file (RF), 0 to n records for each title returned by the customer, also sequenced on customer-no (RCNr) and title-no (RTNr).

Customer–No (RCNr)	Title–No (RTNr)	Quantity (RQ)	Total–Returns (TR)

Calculations

- If there are sales, calculate the value QS per title, and the value ΣTS per customer.
- If there are returns, calculate the value QR per title, and the value ΣTR per customer.
- Calculate the balance: BAL = CBAL + ΣTS — ΣTR.
- Calculate the number of titles sold (ΣQS) and returned (ΣQR) per customer. Where either value is zero, spaces are to be printed in SR.

Error condition

• There is an error where a customer has an entry in SF or RF, but none in CF. A record is written in the ER file.

Full page

• Skip to a new page is to be performed after the 30th title-line of SR. Customer-no (CNr) and customer-name (CN) are to appear in the first title-line after the skip to head-of-form.
• At the head of each page, a heading (HD) is to be printed, with a right-justified page number (PG).

Construct the Logical Output File and check your solution against that on the following page before continuing. Do not neglect the case $\overline{\text{OUTPUT}}$, even if you find that the set is empty. Include, where appropriate, the actions which produce output.

Logical Output File

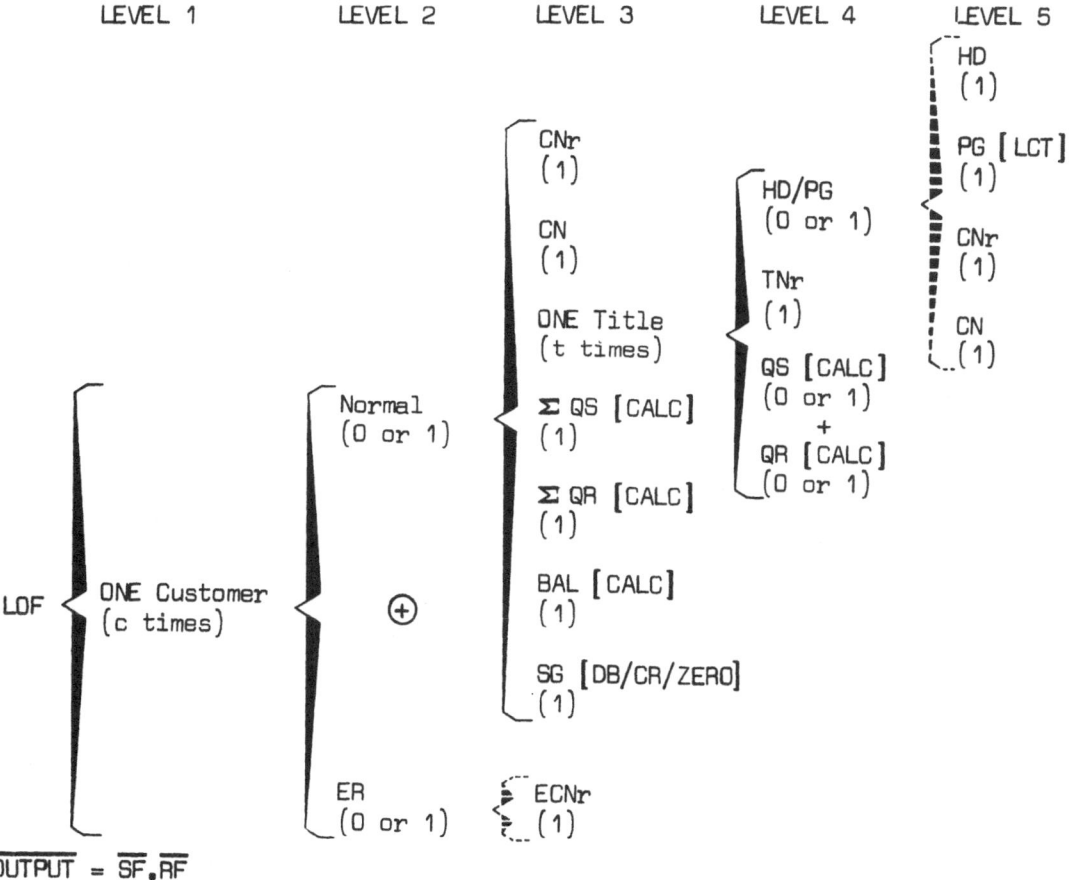

$\overline{\text{OUTPUT}} = \overline{\text{SF}}.\overline{\text{RF}}$

Now construct the Logical Input File and any Logical Phase Files and truth tables you find to be required.

Logical Input File

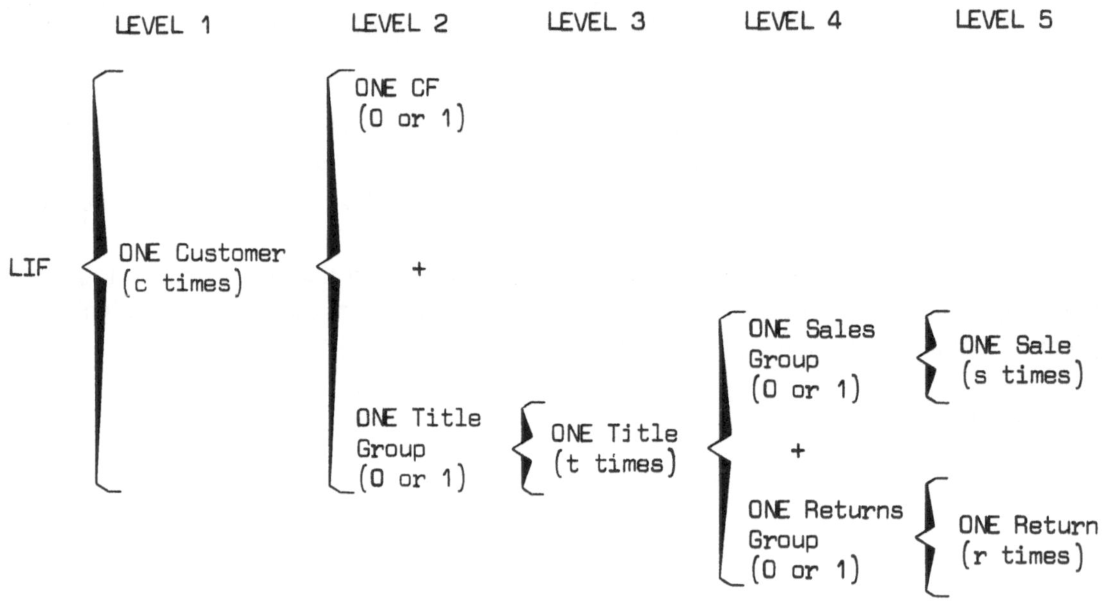

	LEVEL 1	LEVEL 2	LEVEL 3	LEVEL 4	LEVEL 5

LIF
{
ONE Customer (c times)
{
ONE CF (0 or 1)

+

ONE Title Group (0 or 1)
{
ONE Title (t times)
{
ONE Sales Group (0 or 1)
{
ONE Sale (s times)

+

ONE Returns Group (0 or 1)
{
ONE Return (r times)

Logical Phase Files

LPF2
{
ONE Customer C.F.
{
BAL [< 0: 0/1]

+

BAL [$\overline{<0}$: 0/1]

LPF3
{
ONE Title
{
LCT [=30: 0/1]

C = CF Record; T = Titles group.

Tables

ONE Customer C T	ER See Table 3	$\overline{\text{OUTPUT}}$	See Table 2
0 0	Ϙ	Ϙ	Ϙ
0 1	X		
1 0		X	
1 1			X

Table 1: C = CF record; T = Titles group.

ONE C.T Customer S R	Process S	Process R
0 0	Ϙ	Ϙ
0 1		X
1 0	X	
1 1	X	X

Table 2: S = Sales group; R = Returns group.

ONE $\overline{\text{CF}}$ Customer S R	GET SF	GET RF
0 0	Ϙ	Ϙ
0 1		X
1 0	X	
1 1	X	X

Table 3:

ONE C.T Customer <0 >0	SG = ZERO	SG = DB	SG = CR
0 0	X		
0 1			X
1 0		X	
1 1	Ϙ	Ϙ	Ϙ

Table 4: < 0 = debit balance; > 0 = credit balance.

Now analyze the program into logical sequences, and draw up its flowchart.

Logical sequences

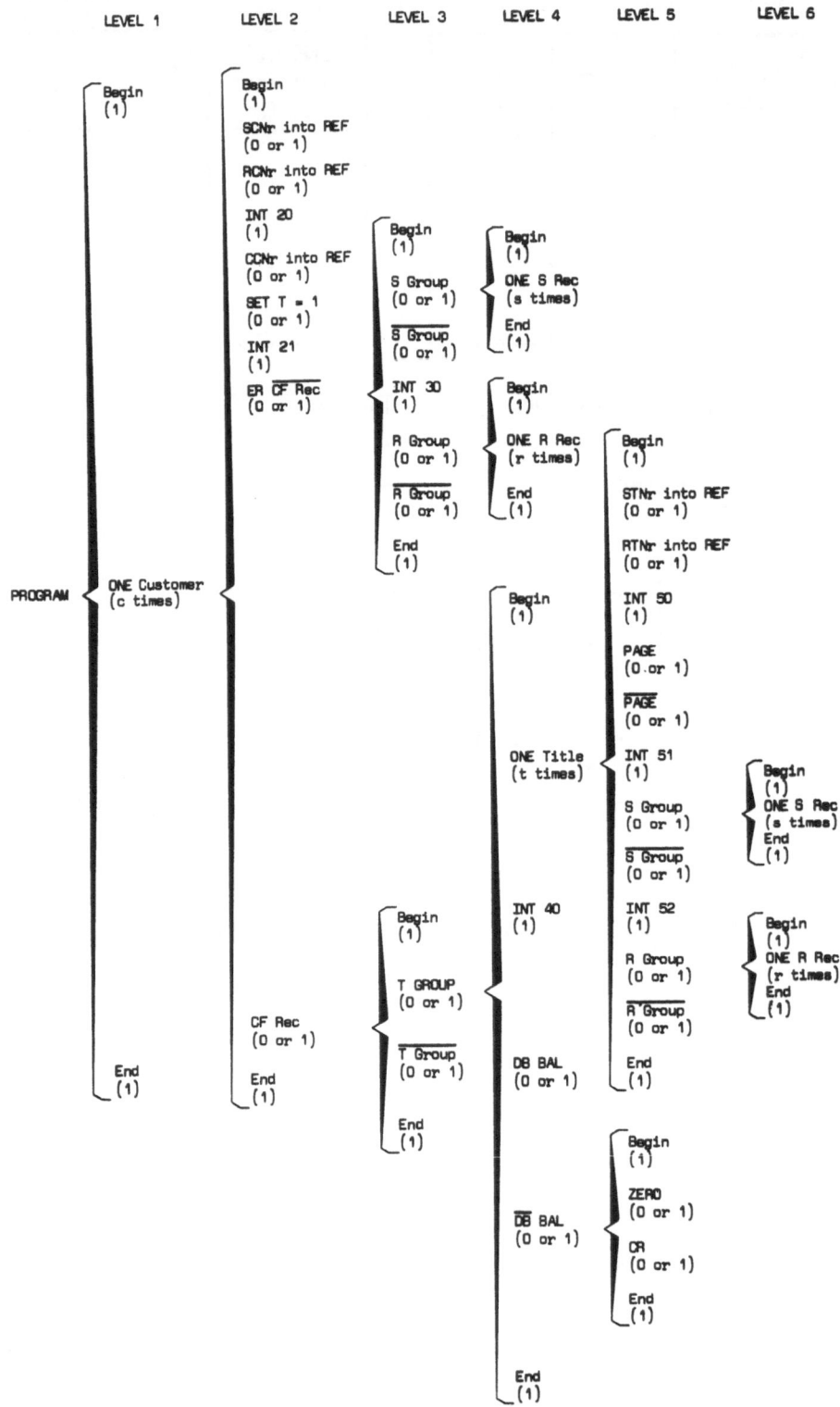

Flowchart to level 4

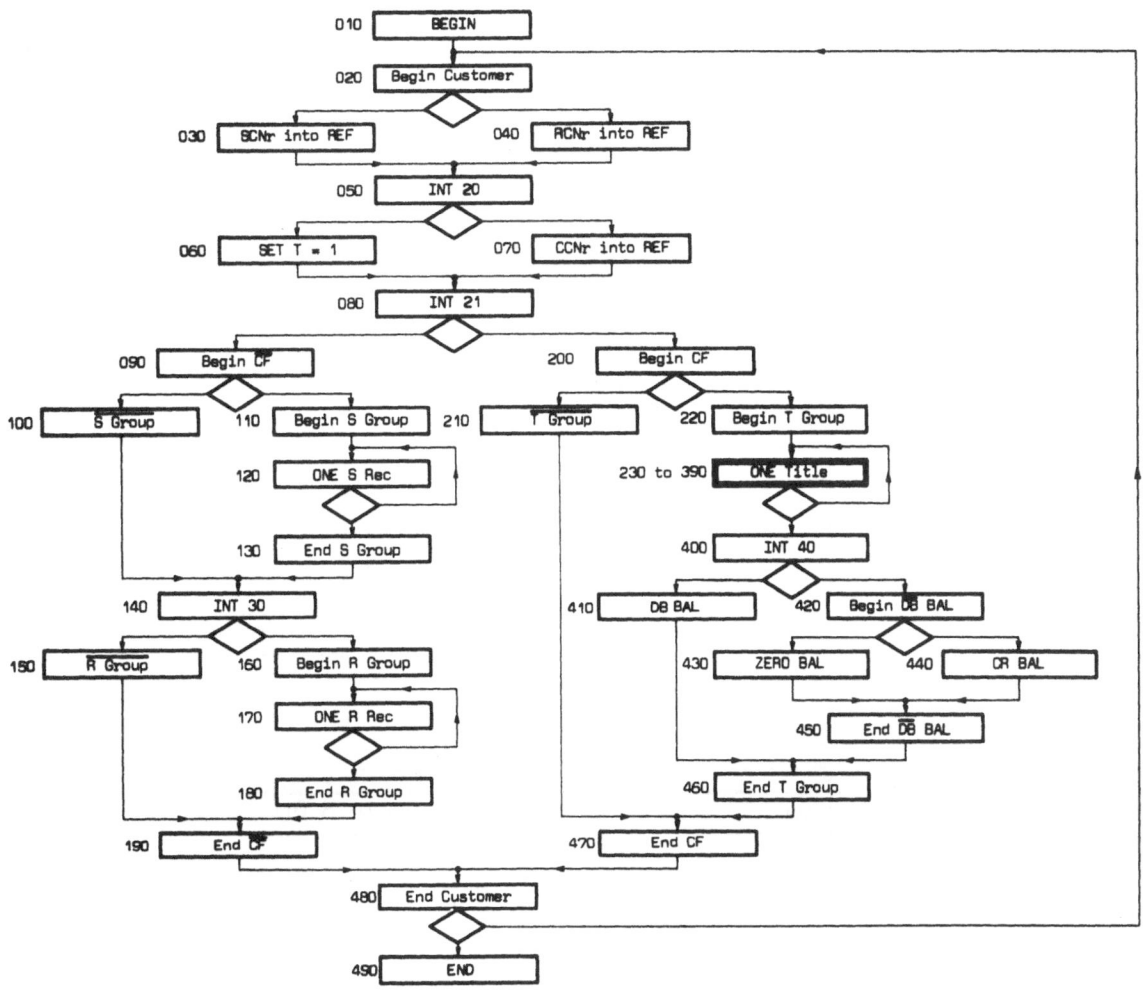

Flowchart of logical sequences for processing a title

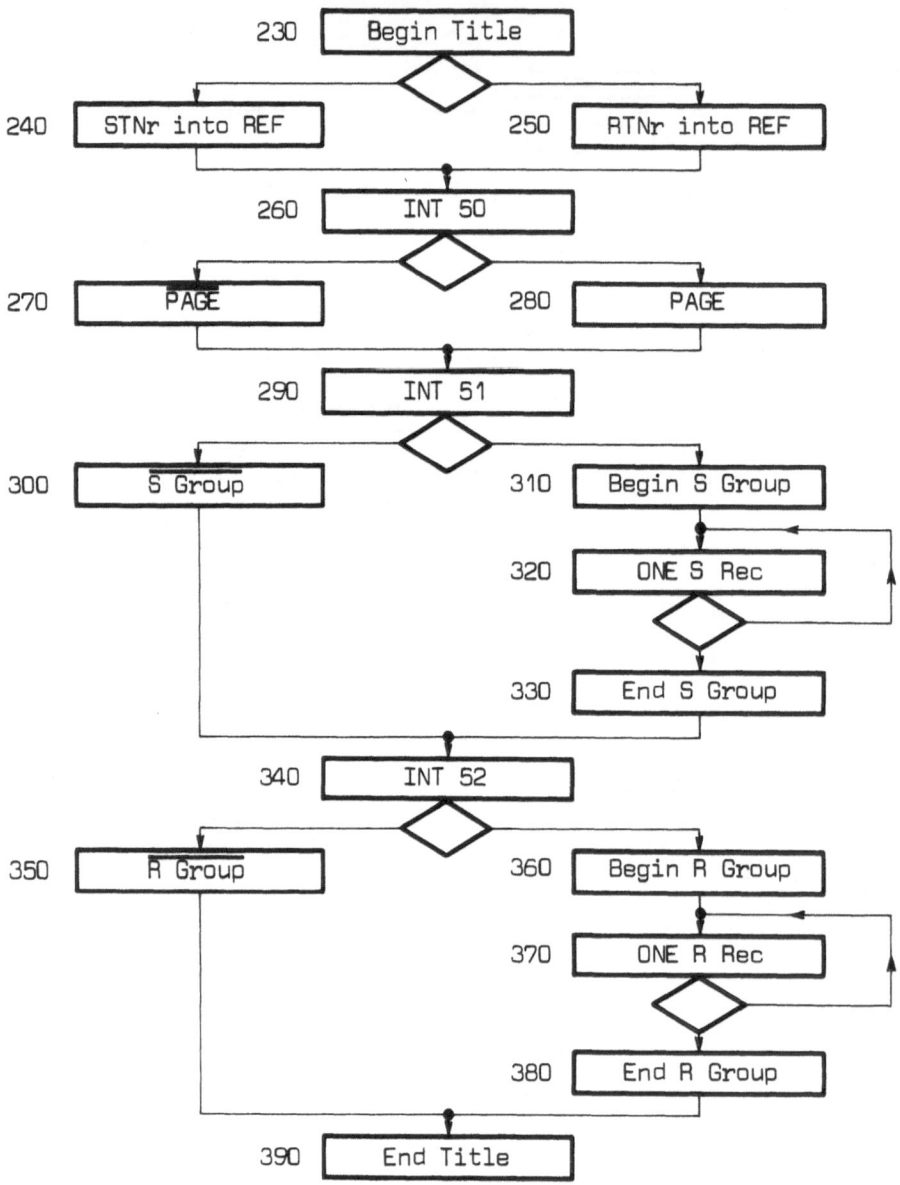

Now organize the details of the program.

- Construct the list of instructions by categories, so as to check the mapping of the set of instructions to the set of logical sequences.
- Construct the sequenced list of instructions.

Check your solution using the LOF, before comparing it to the solution proposed on the next page.

List of instructions by category

In the following list, the reference areas (REF) are distinguished into CRF (customer reference), TRF (title reference), and CTRF (combining the two).

```
010 GET CF                                                              230
470 GET CF                          400 IF D̄B̄                          420
010 GET SF                          410                                 460
120 GET SF                          420 IF CR                           440
320 GET SF                          430                                 440
010 GET RF                          480 IF ēōf̄                          020
170 GET RF
370 GET RF                          030 SCNr into CRF
                                    040 RCNr into CRF
020 IF RCNr < SCNr       040        070 CCNr into CRF
030                      050        060 T = 1
050 IF CCNr < CRFNr      070        020 T = 0
060                      080        250 RTNr into TRF
080 IF CCNr = CRFNr      200        240 STNr into TRF
090 IF SCNr = CRFNr      110        010 LCT = 30
100                      140        280 INIT LCT
120 IF SCNr = CRFNr      120        390 LCT + 1
140 IF RCNr = CRFNr      160        460 LCT + 1
150                      190
170 IF RCNr = CRFNr      170        310 QS = 0
190                      480        360 QR = 0
200 IT T = 1             220        220 ΣQS = 0
210                      470        220 ΣQR = 0
230 IF RTNr < STNr       250        320 QS + SQ
240                      260        370 QR + RQ
260 IF LCT = 30          280        330 ΣQS + QS
270                      290        380 ΣQR + QR
290 IF STNr = CTRFNr     310        220 CBAL into CAL
300                      340        320 CAL + TS
                                    370 CAL — TR
320 IF STNr = CTRFNr     320        010 PG = 1
340 IF RTNr = CTRFNr     360        280 PG + 1
350                      390        190 FMT ER
370 IF RTNr = CTRFNr     370        190 PUT ER
390 IF (SCNr = CRFNr). (RCNr = CRFNr)   220 FMT CCNr, CCN in WRK
```

290 FMT TNr	280 PUT SR & INIT
330 FMT QS	280 FMT CNr, CN
380 FMT QR	400 FMT Totals-Line
390 WRK into SR	410 FMT DB in SG
390 PUT SR & INIT	440 FMT CR in SG
390 INIT WRK	430 FMT ZERO in SG
280 FMT HOF	460 PUT SR & INIT

Sequenced list of instructions

Line	Instruction	Ref
010	LCT = 30	
	PG = 1	
	GET CF	
	GET SF	
	GET RF	
020	T = 0	
	IF RCNr < SCNr	040
030	SCNr into CRF	050
040	RCNr into ÇRF	
050	IF CCNr < CRFNr	070
060	T = 1	080
070	CCNr into CRF	
080	IF CCNr = CRFNr	200
090	IF SCNr = CRFNr	110
100		140
110		
120	GET SF	
	IF SCNr = CRFNr	120
130		
140	IF RCNr = CRFNr	160
150		190
160		
170	GET RF	
	IF RCNr = CRFNr	170
180		
190	FMT ER	
	PUT ER	480
200	IF T = 1	220
210		470
220	ΣQS = 0	
	ΣQR = 0	
	CEAL into CAL	
	CNr, CN into WRK	
230	IF RTNr < STNr	250
240	STNr into TRF	260
250	RTNr into TRF	
260	IF LCT = 30	280
270		290
280	INIT LCT	
	PG + 1	
	FMT HOF	

Line	Instruction	Ref
	PUT SR & INIT	
	FMT CNr, CN	
290	FMT TNr	
	IF STNr = CTRFNr	310
300		340
310	QS = 0	
320	QS + SQ	
	CAL + TS	
	GET SF	
	IF STNr = CTRFNr	320
330	ΣQS + QS	
	FMT QS	
340	IF RTNr = CTRFNr	360
350		390
360	QR = 0	
370	QR + RQ	
	CAL — TR	
	GET RF	
	IF RTNr = CTRFNr	370
380	ΣQR + QR	
	FMT QR	
390	LCT + 1	
	WRK into SR	
	PUT SR & INIT	
	INIT WRK	
	IF (SCNr = CRFNr). (RCNr = CRFNr)	230
400	FMT Totals-Line	
	IF $\overline{DB}$	420
410	FMT DB	460
420	IF CR	440
430	FMT ZERO	450
440	FMT CR	
450		
460	LCT + 1	
	PUT SR & INIT	
470	GET CF	
480	IF $\overline{EOF}$	020
490		END

MODIFICATION PROBLEM I

At the same time as the first report, a second report is to be produced with one line for each customer having an entry in CF, for whom any of the following conditions are met:

- There is a debit balance.
- There were no sales during the year.
- Or both.

Format for Report 2 (SR 2)

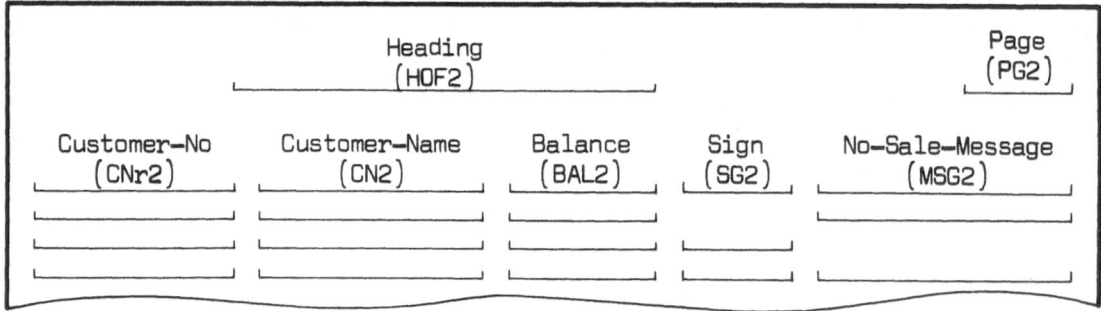

Modify the LOF and (if needed) the LIF; then compare your solution with that given on the following page.

Logical Output File

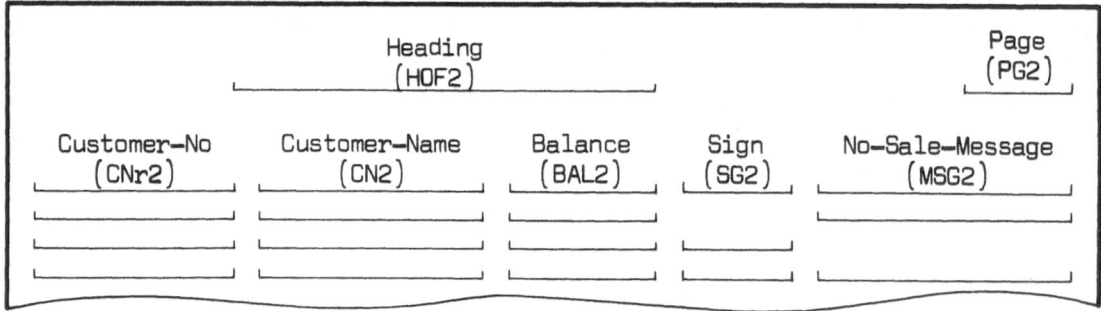

$$\overline{\text{OUTPUT}} = \varphi$$

Logical Input File

$$\text{LIF} \left\{ \begin{array}{l} \text{ONE Customer} \\ \text{(c times)} \end{array} \right. \left\{ \begin{array}{l} \text{ONE CF Rec} \\ \text{(0 or 1)} \end{array} \right. \left\{ \text{CBAL } [<0 : 0/1] \right.$$

LEVEL 1   LEVEL 2   LEVEL 3

Phases

R2 = 1 signals that SR2 is to be produced; D = 1 that there is a debit balance; and S = 0 that there were no sales during the year.

$$\text{LPF4} \left\{ \text{ONE } \overline{\overline{\text{ER}}} \text{ Customer} \left\{ \text{R2 } [=1: 0/1] \left\{ \begin{array}{l} \text{D } [=1: 0/1] \\ \overline{\text{S}} \ [=1: 0/1] \end{array} \right. \right. \right.$$

$$\text{LPF5} \left\{ \text{LCT2 } [=20: 0/1] \right.$$

Phase 4 R2 = 1 D S	FMT SG2	FMT MSG2
0 0	φ	φ
0 1		X
1 0	X	
1 1	X	X

Revise the subdivision of the program into logical sequences (i.e. redefine set P1). Redraw the flow-chart, omitting sequence numbers; then check the proposed solution and adopt the numbering used there.

Subdivision into logical sequences

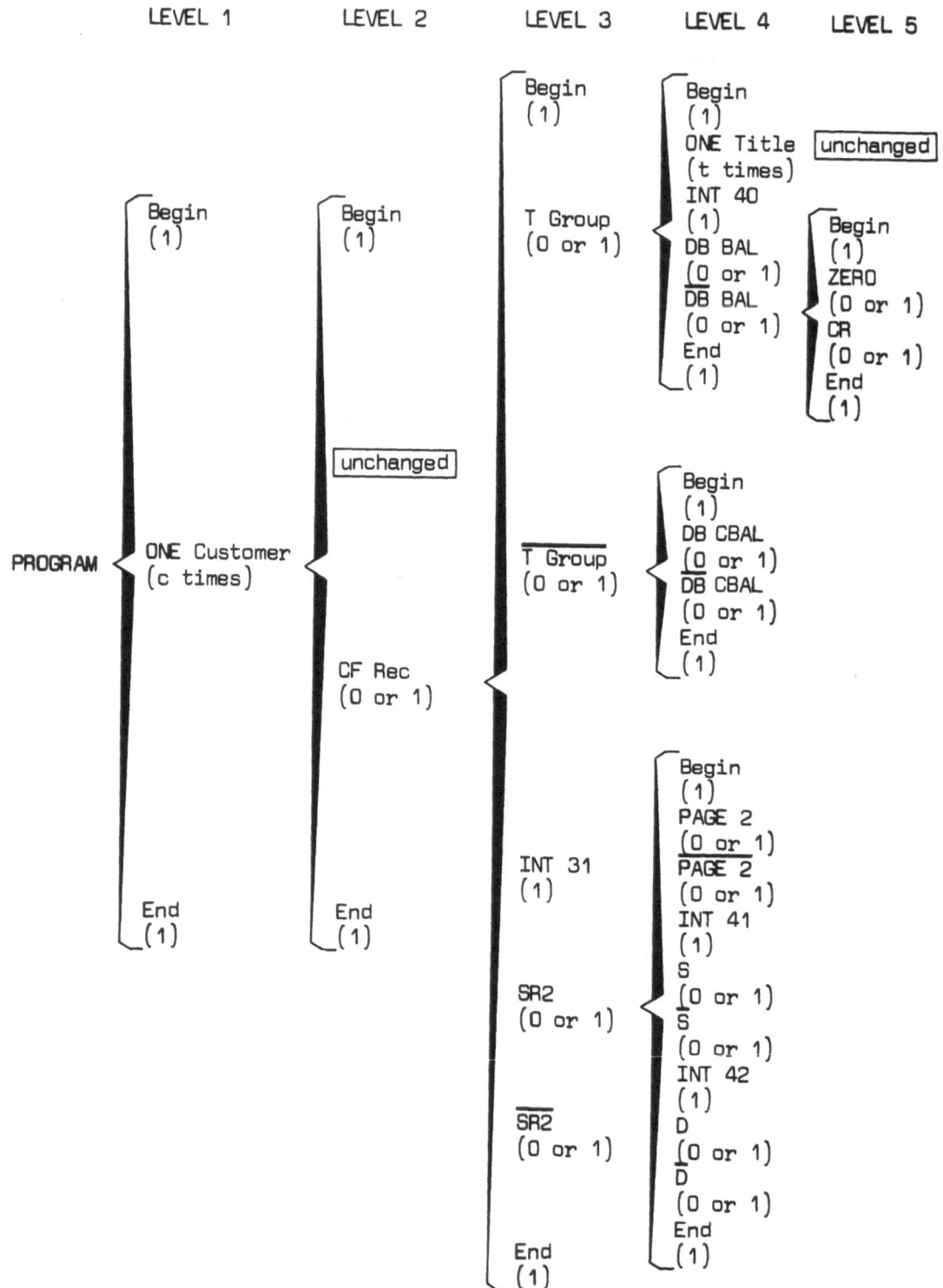

Flowchart of the modified program

Since it is unchanged, the flowchart for the title-processing subset is omitted here.

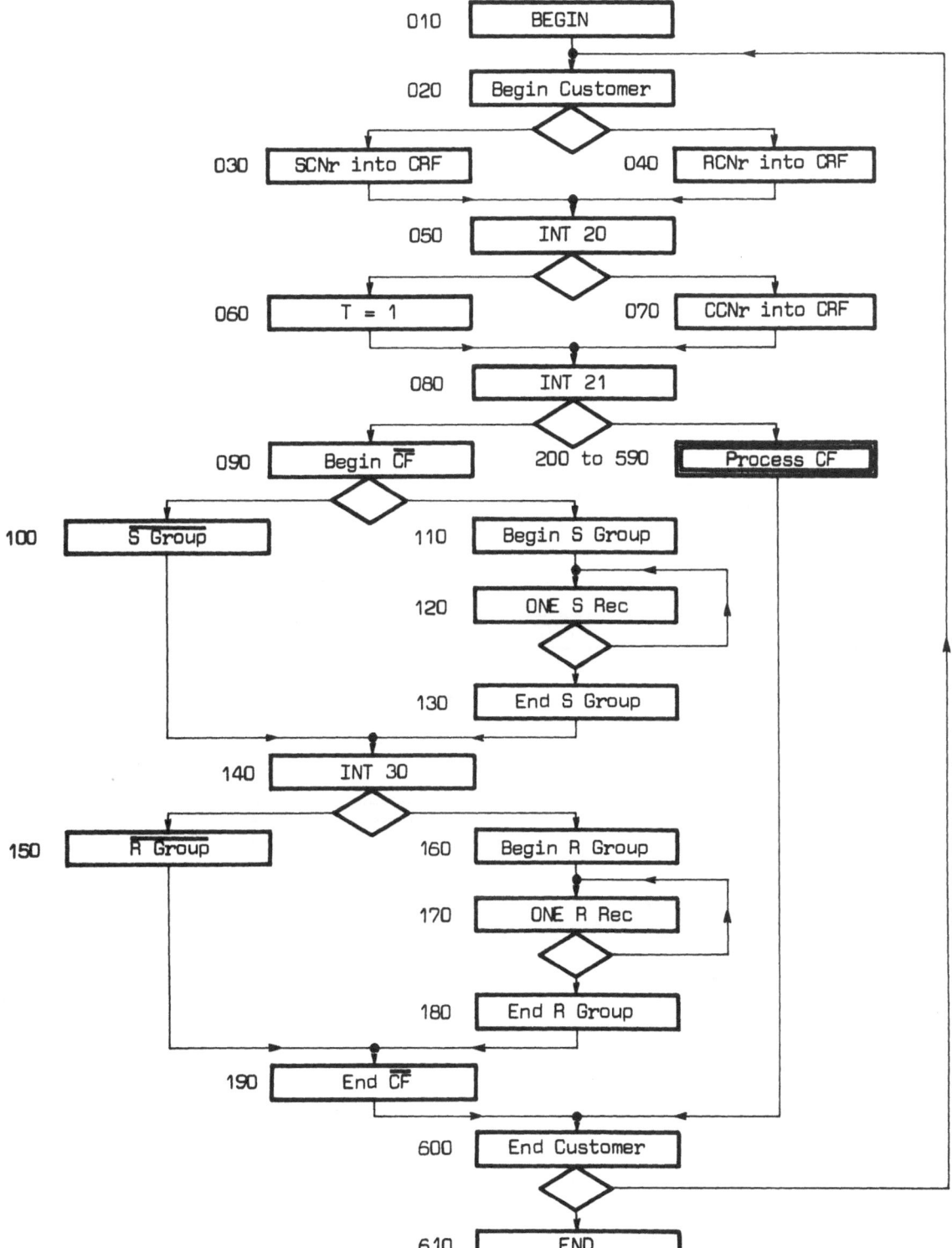

Program Modification

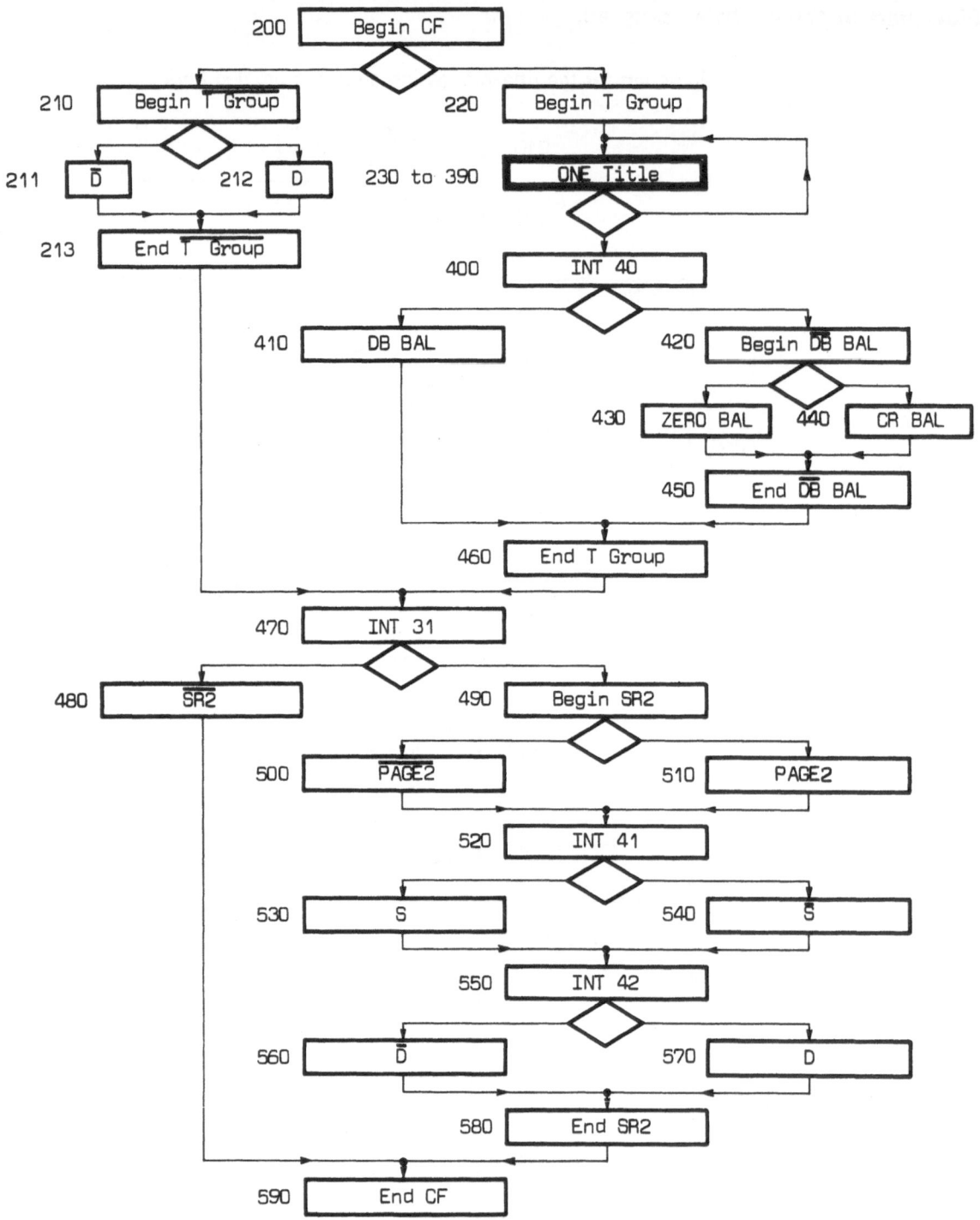

Now construct the list of instructions, by category, to be added to the program.

List by category of instructions to be added to the program

210 IF CBAL < 0	212
211	213
470 IF R2 = 1	490
480	590
490 IF LCT2 = 20	510
500	520
520 IF S = 0	540
530	550
550 IF D = 1	570
560	580
600 IF $\overline{EOF}$	020

```
310 R2 = 0
200 R2 = 1
410 R2 = 1
010 LCT2 = 20
510 LCT2 = 0
580 LCT2 + 1
330 S = 0
200 S = 1
200 D = 0
212 D = 1
410 D = 1

010 PG2 = 1
510 PG2 + 1

510 FMT HOF 2
510 PUT SR 2 & INIT
520 FMT SR 2
570 FMT SG 2 (SG 2 = DB)
540 FMT MSG 2
580 PUT SR 2 & INIT
```

Since the number of modifications is so large, reconstruct the entire sequenced list of program instructions.

Complete sequenced list of instructions for the modified program

Line	Instruction	Jump		Line	Instruction	Jump
010	LCT 2 = 20				ΣQR	
	LCT = 30				CBAL into CAL	
	PG = 1				CNr, CN into WRK	
	PG 2 = 1			230	IF RTNr < STNr	250
	GET CF			240	STNr into TRF	260
	GET SF			250	RTNr into TRF	
	GET R			260	IF LCT = 30	280
020	T = 0			270		290
	IF RCNr < SCNr	040		280	INIT LCT	
030	SCNr into CRF	050			PG + 1	
040	RCNr into CRF				FMT HOF	
050	IF CCNr < CRFNr	070			PUT SR & INIT	
060	T = 1				FMT CNr, CN	
070	CCNr into CRF			290	FMT TNr	
080	IF CCNr = CRFNr	200			IF STNr = CTRFNr	310
090	IF SCNr = CRFNr	110		300		340
100		140		310	QS = 0	
110					R2 = 0	
120	GET SF			320	QS + SQ	
	IF SCNr = CRFNr	120			CAL + TS	
130					GET SF	
140	IF RCNr = CRFNr	160			IF STNr = CTRFNr	320
150		190		330	S = 0	
160					ΣQS + QS	
170	GET RF				FMT QS	
	IF RCNr = CRFNr	170		340	IF RTNr = CTRFNr	360
180				350		390
190	FMT ER			360	QR = 0	
	PUT ER	480		370	QR + RQ	
200	R 2 = 1				CAL — TR	
	S = 1				GET RF	
	D = 0				IF RTNr = CTRFNr	370
	IF T = 1	220		380	ΣQR + QR	
210	IF CBAL < 0	212			FMT QR	
211		213		390	LCT + 1	
212	D = 1				WRK into SR	
213		470			PUT SR & INIT	
220	ΣQS				INIT WRK	

	IF (SCNr = CRFNr).(RCNr = CRFNr) 230				PG2 + 1	
400	FMT Totals-Line				FMT HOF 2	
	IF D = 0	420			PUT SR 2 & INIT	
410	R 2 = 1			520	FMT SR 2	
	D = 1				IF S = 0	540
	FMT SG1	460		530		550
420	IF CR	440		540	FMT MSG 2	
430	FMT ZERO			550	IF D = 1	570
440	FMT CR			560		580
450				570	PUT SR 2 & INIT	
460	LCT + 1				FMT SG 2 (SG2 = DB)	
	PUT SR & INIT			580	LCT2 + 1	
470	IF R2 = 1	490			PUT SR 2 & INIT	
480		590		590	GET CF	
490	IF LCT2 = 20	510		600	IF $\overline{EOF}$	020
500		520		610		END
510	LCT2 = 0					

MODIFICATION PROBLEM 2

There is a request for a new modification in the first report, touching only on those customers for whom no error condition was detected. At the end of the report, on a separate, untitled page, it is desired to have in two lines some general totals for the year.

Abbreviations:

- G ΣQT.$\overline{S}$ Number of titles for which there were returns and no sales.
- G ΣQT.S Number of titles for which there were sales, whether or not there were returns.
- G ΣQT.$\overline{R}$ Number of titles with no returns for which there were sales.
- G ΣQT.R Number of titles for which there were returns, whether or not there were sales.
- G ΣQC.S Number of copies (of all titles) sold (by all bookstores).
- G ΣQC.R Number of copies returned.

Make the desired modifications in the LOF, then see what changes are required in the input files and in the set of logical sequences Pl. Then carry out the detailed organization of the program: redefinition of the set of program instructions Pi. Compare your solution with that given below after having checked it against the LOF.

Logical Output File

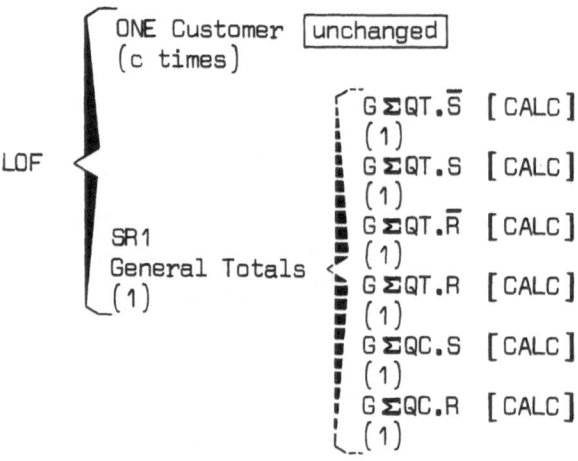

There is no modification to be made in the LIF or in any LPF, so the set Pl does not have to be redefined. Only set Pi is to be modified. You will note that the logic of the program would have had to be altered if we had not followed the logical principles outlined earlier in this book.

Instructions to be added to the program

010 INIT G ΣQT. $\overline{S}$	350 G ΣQT. $\overline{R}$ + 1
010 INIT G ΣQT. S	360 G ΣQT. R + 1
010 INIT G ΣQT. $\overline{R}$	400 G ΣQC. S + QS
010 INIT G ΣQT. R	400 G ΣQC. R + QR
010 INIT G ΣQC. S	610 PAGE 1
010 INIT G ΣQC. R	610 FMT G QT-Line
300 G ΣQT. $\overline{S}$ + 1	610 PUT SR 1 & INIT
310 G ΣQT. S + 1	610 FMT G QC-Line
	610 PUT SR 1 & INIT

MODIFICATION PROBLEM 3

A separate page is to be added to the second report.

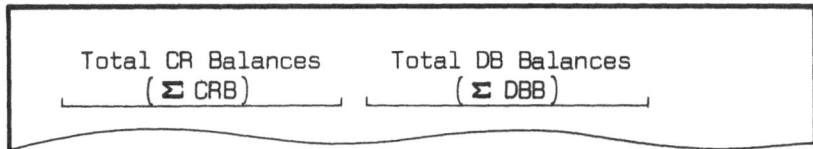

Make the necessary modifications.

Logical Output File

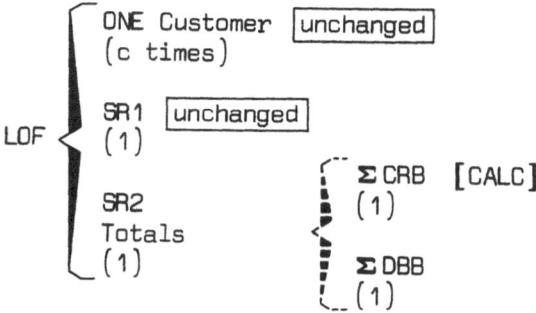

Once again the input (LIF, LPF) remains unchanged and the set of logical sequences PI needs no alteration. Only the set of instructions Pi is to be redefined.

Instructions to be added to the program

```
010 ΣCRB = 0
010 ΣDBB = 0
211 ΣCRB + CBAL
440 ΣCRB + BAL
540 ΣDBB + BAL
610 PAGE 2
610 FMT ΣCRB, ΣDBB
610 PUT SR 2 & INIT
```

Did you correctly program the calculations for CR balance?

3 — FILE UPDATE

PROBLEM

A magazine subscription file is to be updated.

Program Diagram

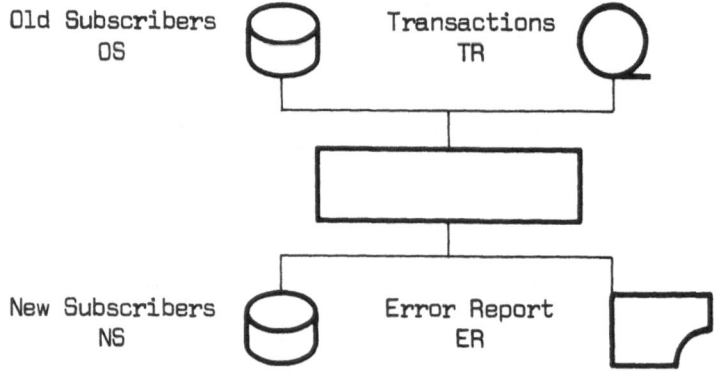

Outputs

New-Subscribers file (NS), 0 or 1 record per subscriber; 0 if error.

Subscription–No (NSNr)	Name/Address (NNA)	Subscription–Date (NSD)	Expiration–Date (NED)

Error-Report file (ER), 0 or 1 record per subscriber; 1 if error.

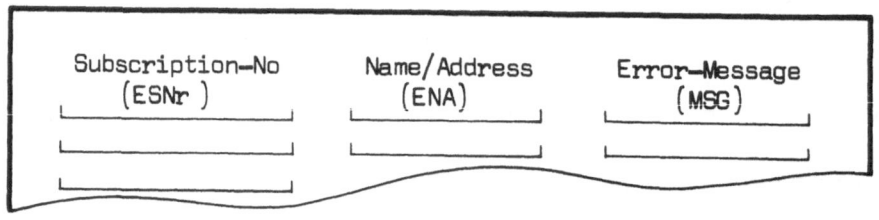

Inputs

Old-Subscribers file (OS), 0 or 1 record per subscriber; sequenced on ascending subscription-numbers.

Subscription–No (OSNr)	Name/Address (ONA)	Subscription–Date (OSD)	Expiration–Date (OED)

Transaction file (TR), 0 or 1 record per subscriber, sequenced on subscription-numbers.

Subscription No (TSNr)	Name/Address (TNA)	Subscription–Date (TSD)	Expiration–Date (TED)	Code (C)

C may have one of several values.

      C = 0   Cancel old subscription.
      C = 1   Modify old subscription.
      C = 2   Enter new subscription.

Constants:

- Current date (CD).
- Error-message texts (MSG).

Processing

If $OS.\overline{TR}$, the OS record is to be duplicated in NS, provided the expiration date OED has not passed; otherwise the record is omitted from NS.

If there is a transaction (TR), processing depends on the value of C.

- $\overline{OS}.TR$ and C = 2:   Create a new NS record.
- OS.TR and C = 0:   Cancel OS record.
- OS.TR and C = 1:   Alter OS record in NS.

Errors:

- $\overline{OS}.TR$ and C = 1:   Alteration with no OS record.
- $\overline{OS}.TR$ and C = 0:   Cancellation with no OS record.
- OS.TR and C = 2:   Creation with existing OS record.
- C = other value: Code error.

Where the subscription-record is altered, the expiration date in the corresponding TR record is to be checked; if the date is past, the record is to be eliminated from NS. A preceding program has eliminated the case of new-record creation with a past expiration date.

Establish the logical output and input files, and describe the conditions for $\overline{\text{OUTPUT}}$. Check your solution against ours before proceeding further.

Where a code may have more than three values, it may be simpler to express it in the following manner.

   C (= 0, 1, 2, other: 0 or 1).

It then becomes superfluous to construct a truth table, since the corresponding program is still tree-structured.

Logical Output File

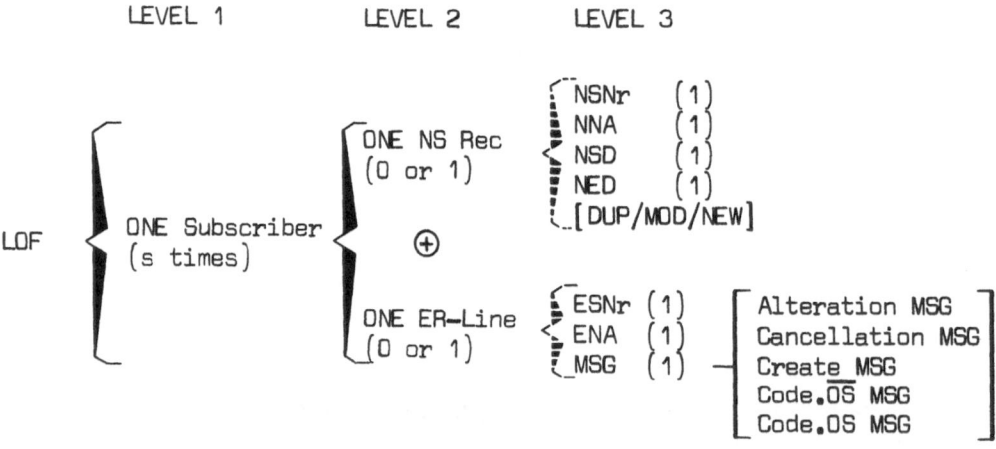

$$\overline{\text{OUTPUT}} = \text{Subscriber} \left[\text{OS.TR.C=0} + \text{CD} > \text{ED} \right]$$

Logical Input File

	LEVEL 1	LEVEL 2	LEVEL 3
LIF	ONE Subscriber (s times)	ONE OS Rec (0 or 1)	OED [< CD: 0/1]
		+	
		ONE TR Rec (0 or 1)	TED [<CD:0/1] + C [= 0, 1, 2, other : 0/1]

Now construct the truth tables for the subdivision of the program into logical sequences for the first three levels, and draw the corresponding program flowchart. Do not number the sequences yet. Then check the proposed solution with those given below.

Table 1 of Level 2.

OS = Old-Subscribers record; TR = Transaction record.

ONE Subscriber			See Table $OS.\overline{TR}$	See Table $\overline{OS}.TR$	See Table $OS.TR$
	OS	TR			
0	0	0	⣉	⣉	⣉
1	0	1		X	
2	1	0	X		
3	1	1			X

Table 1 of Level 3.

ONE $OS.\overline{TR}$ Subscriber TED < CD	OS into NS PUT NS	CNCL
0	X	
1		X

Logical Sequences

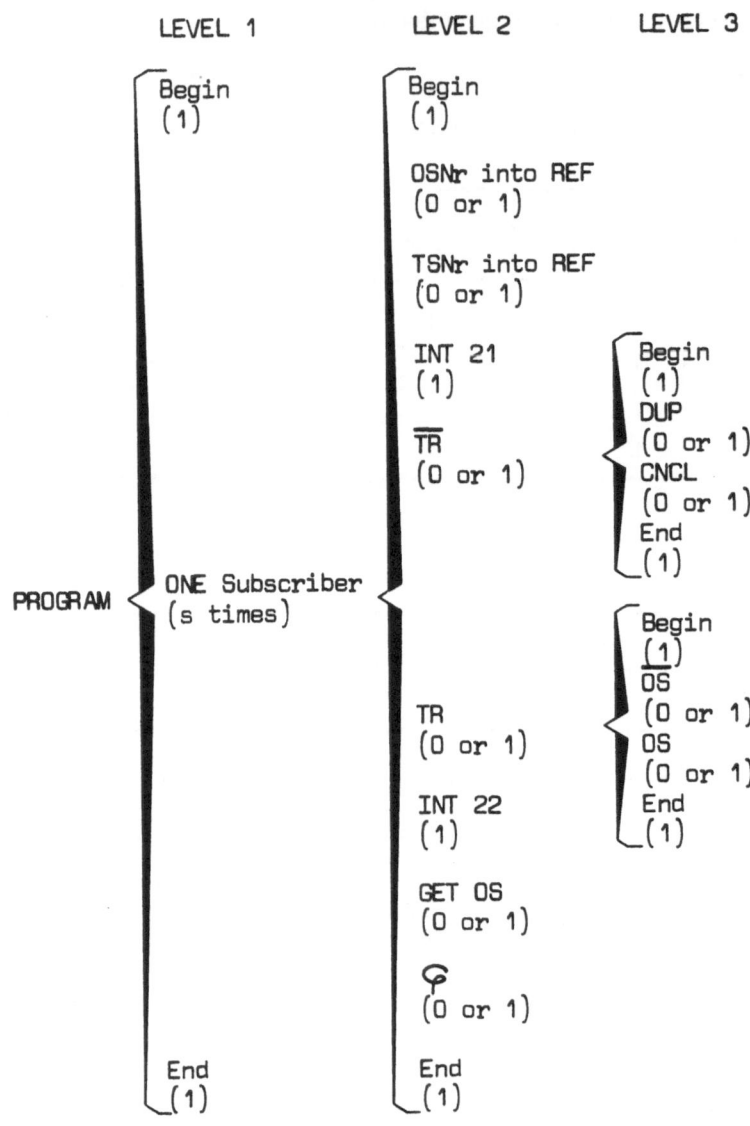

Flowchart to Level 3

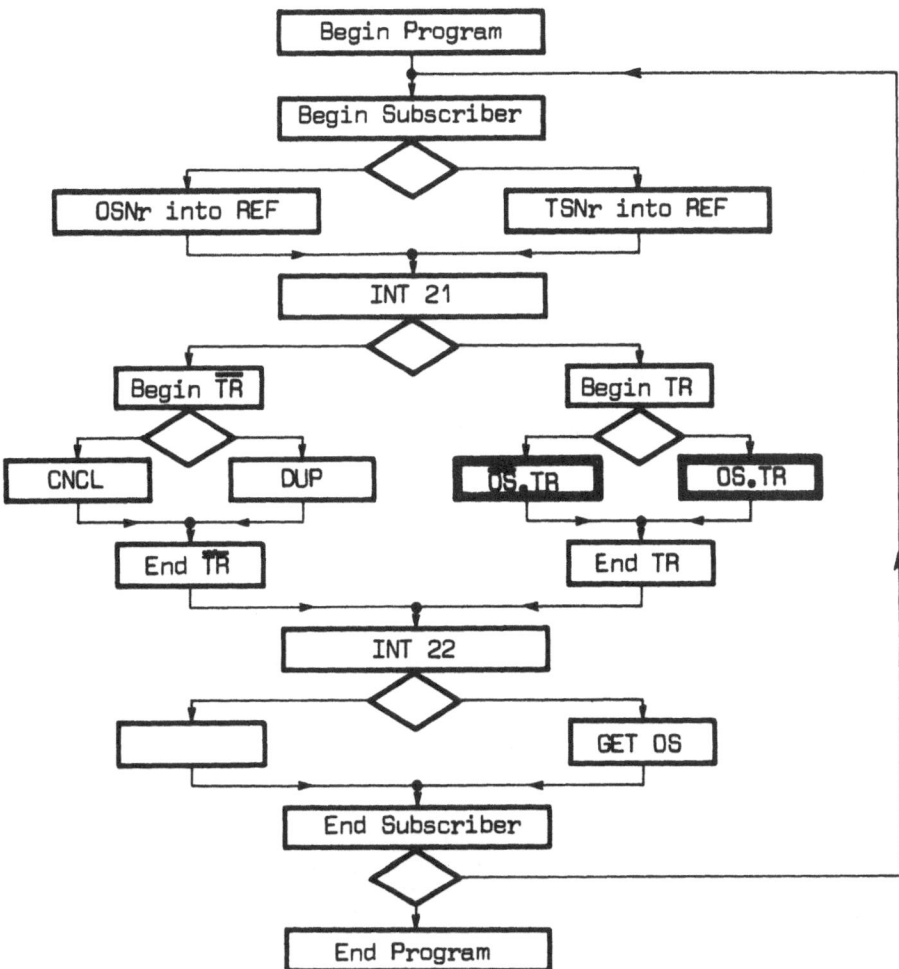

Now organize the two subsets $\overline{OS}$.TR and OS.TR, giving their logical-sequence diagrams. Check your answer before continuing.

Subset $\overline{OS}$.TR

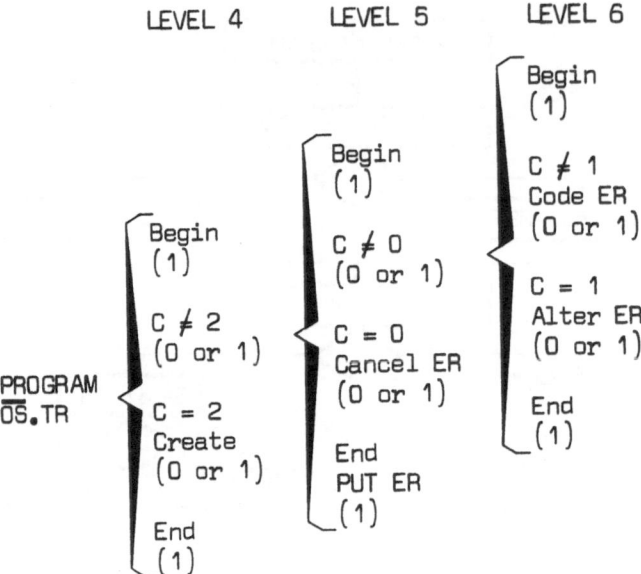

Subset OS.TR

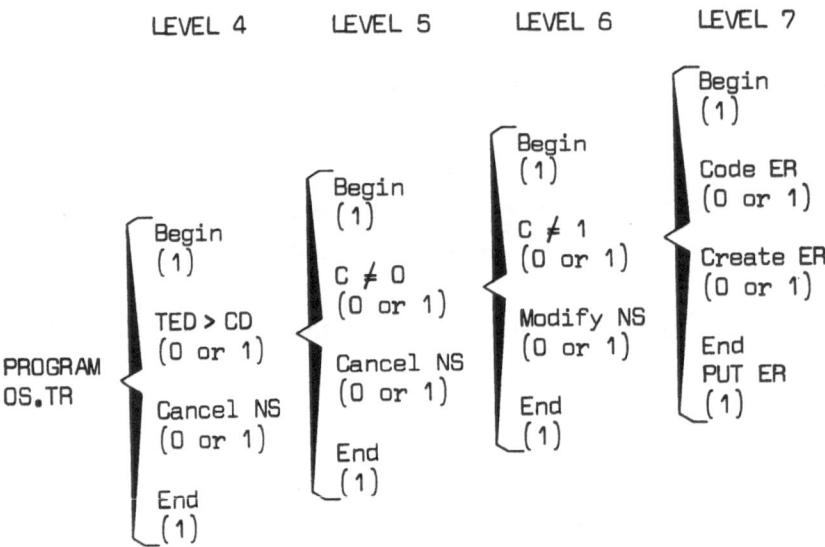

Rework the flowchart for level 3, and then those for the subsets OS.TR and OS.TR. Assign numbers to the logical sequences, then check your answer, first against the LOF, then against the solution given on the following pages.

Flowchart to Level 3

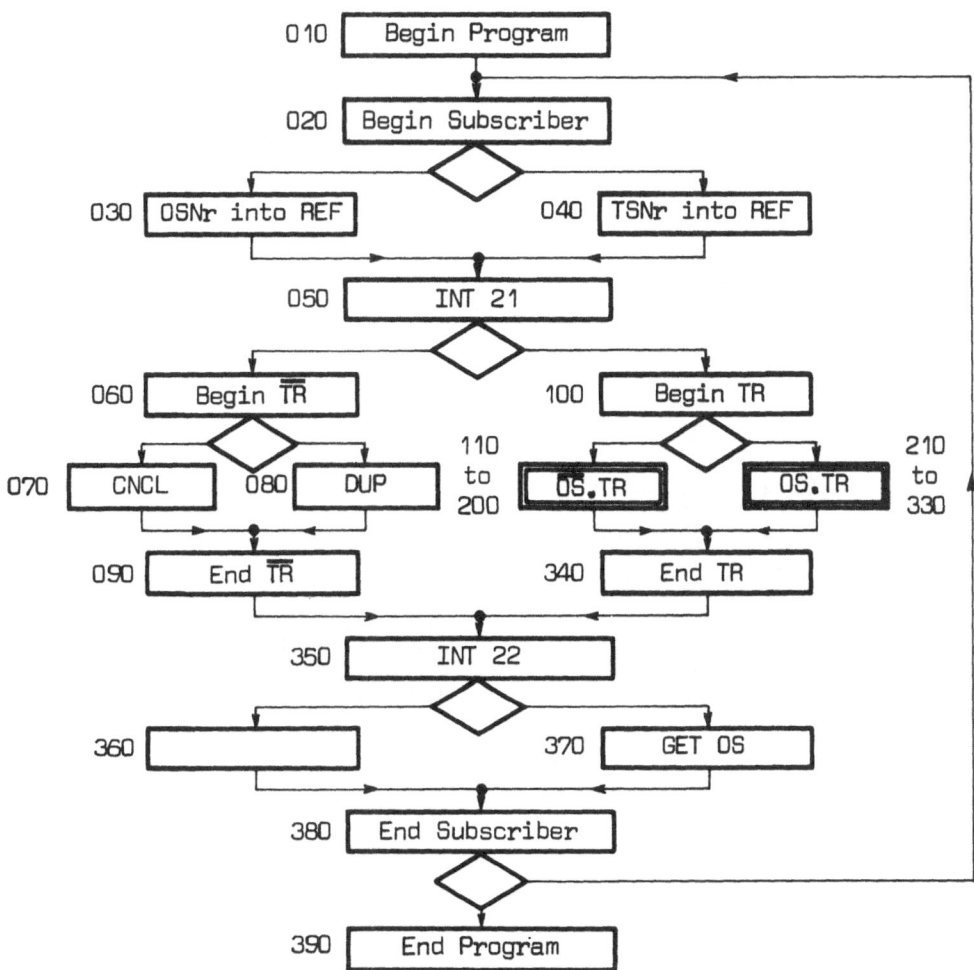

Flowchart for Subset $\overline{OS}$.TR

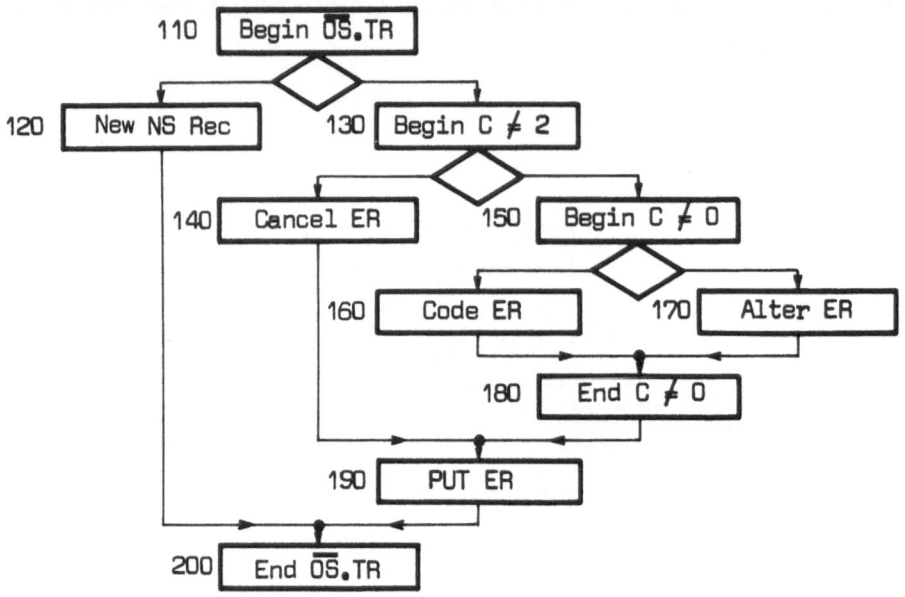

Flowchart for Subset OS.TR

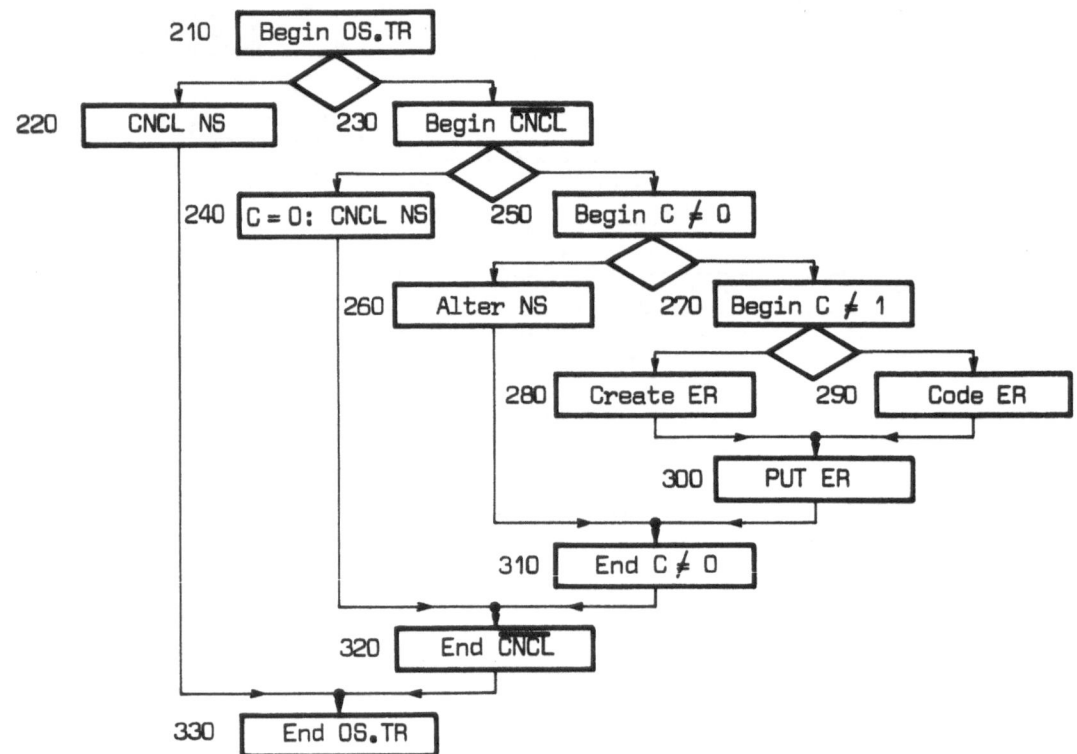

Note that the hierarchical organization of the flowchart provides both a general view of the program in the first flowchart, and a clear picture of the two major subsets, OS.TR and OS.TR.

Now establish the detailed organization by instruction category, followed by the sequenced list of program instructions.

When you have completed the detailed organization, verify your solution using the LOF, the set $\overline{\text{OUTPUT}}$, and the truth tables; then organize a test data set for program checkout.

Instructions by Categories

010 GET OS		
010 GET TR		
340 GET TR		
370 GET OS		
020 IF TSNr < OSNr	040	
030	050	
050 IF TSNr = REFNr	100	
060 IF OED < CD	080	
070	090	
090	350	
100 IF OSNr = REFNr	210	
110 IF C ≠ 2	130	
120	200	
130 IF C ≠ 0	150	
140	190	
150 IF C = 1	170	
160	180	
200	340	
210 IF TED > CD	230	
220	330	
230 IF C ≠ 0	250	
240	320	
250 IF C ≠ 1	270	
260	310	

270 IF C ≠ 2	290
280	300
350 IF OSNr = REFNr	370
360	380
380 IF $\overline{\text{EOF}}$	020
030 OSNr into REF	
040 TSNr into REF	
070 Cancel NS *	
120 TR Rec into NS	
120 PUT NS	
130 FMT ESNr, ENA	
140 FMT Cancel-MSG	
160 FMT Code-MSG	
170 FMT Alter MSG	
190 PUT ER & INIT	
220 Cancel NS *	
240 Cancel NS *	
260 FMT TR Rec in NS	
260 PUT NS	
270 FMT ESNr, ENA	
280 FMT Create-MSG	
290 FMT Code-MSG	
300 PUT ER & INIT	

Did you check that the number of elementary structures is the same as the number of conditional branches, and the number of alternative structures is equal to the number of unconditional branches?

* Cancel NS is one action, logically speaking. It corresponds to *'Do not write'* in sequential access and *'Write after flagging'* in direct access.

Sequential Instruction List

010	GET OS		200			340
	GET TR		210	IF TED > CD		230
020	IF TSNr < OSNr	040	220	Cancel NS *		330
030	OSNr into REF	050	230	IF C ≠ 0		250
040	TSNr into REF		240	Cancel NS *		320
050	IF TSNr = REFNr	100				
060	IF OED > CD	080	250	IF C ≠ 1		270
070	Cancel NS *	090	260	FMT TR Rec into NS		
				PUT NS		
080			270	FMT ESNr, ENA		
090		350		IF C ≠ 2		290
100	IF OSNr = REFNr	210	280	FMT Create–MSG		300
110	IF C ≠ 2	130	290	FMT Code–MSG		
120	FMT TR Rec into NS		300	PUT ER & INIT		
	PUT NS	200	310			
130	FMT ESNr, ENA		320			
	IF C ≠ 0	150	330			
140	FMT Cancel–MSG	190	340	GET TR		
150	IF C = 1	170	350	IF OSNr = REFNr		370
160	FMT Code–MSG	180	360			380
170	FMT Alter–MSG		370	GET OS		
180			380	IF $\overline{EOF}$		020
190	PUT ER & INIT		390			END

MODIFICATION PROBLEM

The following modifications are requested for the program.

Outputs

- **New-Subscribers file (NS)** adds a new field to each record:

NS–record–fields [unchanged]	Balance–Due (NBD)

- **Error-Report (ER)** is unchanged.
- **Overpayments-Report (OR)** is added, with one record for each subscriber with a record in NS who has paid more than the Balance-Due (NBD) amount.

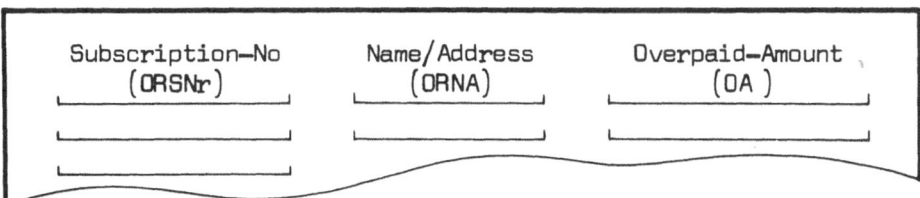

Inputs

- **Old-Subscribers file (OS)** also adds a Balance-Due field.

OS—record—fields [unchanged]	Balance—Due (OBD)

- **Transaction file (TR)** is unchanged.
- **Payments file (PF)** is added, with 0 to n payments per subscriber.

Subscription—No (PSNr)	Amount—Paid (AP)

Processing

Existing processes are unchanged. The following are to be added:

- If there is one or more PF records, calculate ΣAP.
- If there is an NS record, NBD = OBD — ΣAP.
- If NBD < 0, produce an OR record.

Modify the logical output and input files, as well as the definition of the set $\overline{\text{OUTPUT}}$. Then check your solution against that given on the following pages.

Logical Output File

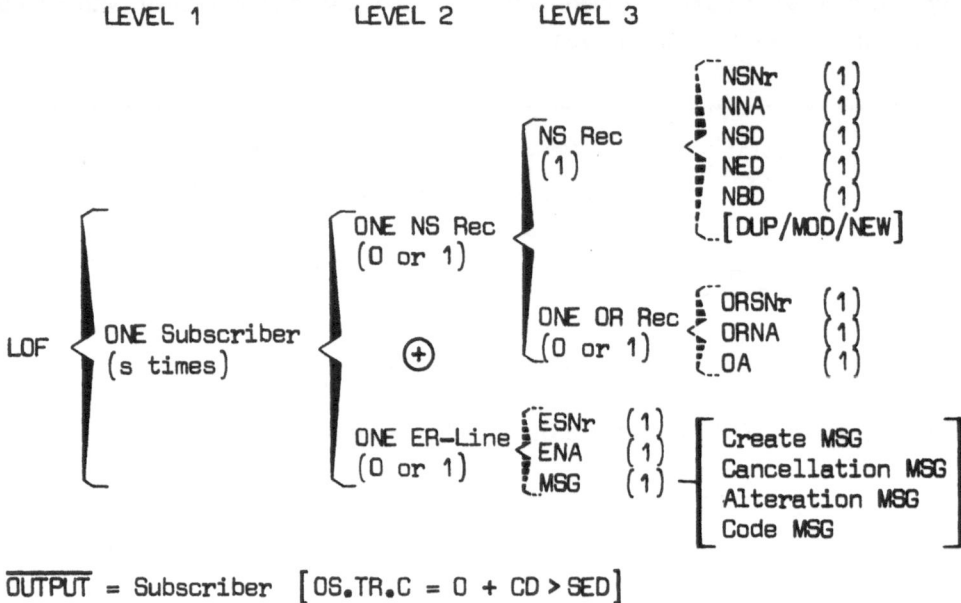

$$\overline{OUTPUT} = Subscriber \; [OS.TR.C = 0 + CD > SED]$$

Logical Input File

```
                 LEVEL 1              LEVEL 2            LEVEL 3

              ┌                    ┌ ONE OS Rec     ┌
              │                    │ (0 or 1)       ┤ OED  [< CD : 0/1]
              │                    │                └
              │                    │    +
      LIF ────┤  ONE Subscriber    ┤ ONE TR Rec     ┌ TED  [< CD : 0/1]
              │  (s times)         │ (0 or 1)       │        +
              │                    │                └ C  [= 0, 1, 2, other : 0/1]
              │                    │
              │                    │ ONE PF Group   ┌ ONE PF Rec
              └                    └ (0 or 1)       └ (p times)
```

Now describe any logical phase files required, revise the truth table for level 2, and draw the corresponding Veitch diagram. Check your solution before continuing.

Logical Phase Files

```
LPF2 { ONE Subscriber { N [= 1 : 0/1]        LPF3 { ONE NS Subscriber { NBD [< 0 : 0/1]
```

Where N = 1 indicates that an NS record is to be produced.

Table 1

ONE SUBSCRIBER			$OS.\overline{TR}$	$\overline{OS}.TR$	$OS.TR$	CALC ΣAP
	OS	TR	PF			
0	0	0	0	φ	φ	φ	φ
1	0	0	1				X
2	0	1	0		X		
3	0	1	1		X		X
4	1	0	0	X			
5	1	0	1	X			X
6	1	1	0			X	
7	1	1	1			X	X

Veitch Diagram

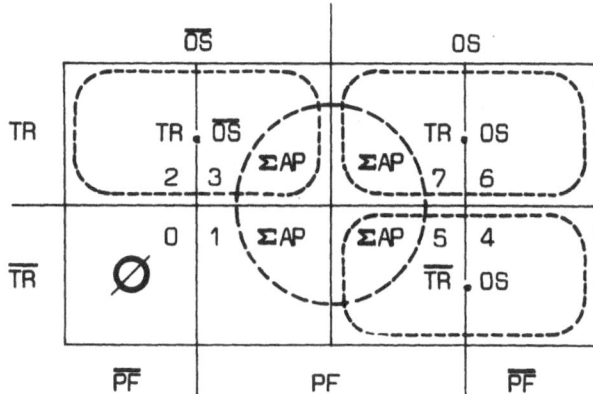

You will have noticed that the parts of the program corresponding to sets $\overline{OS}.TR$, OS.TR, and OS.$\overline{TR}$ remain unchanged.

Now perform the subdivision of the program for the first three levels. Check your solution against the LOF, and against the solution which follows. Pay particular attention to the synchronization of input files.

Program Modification

Logical Sequences

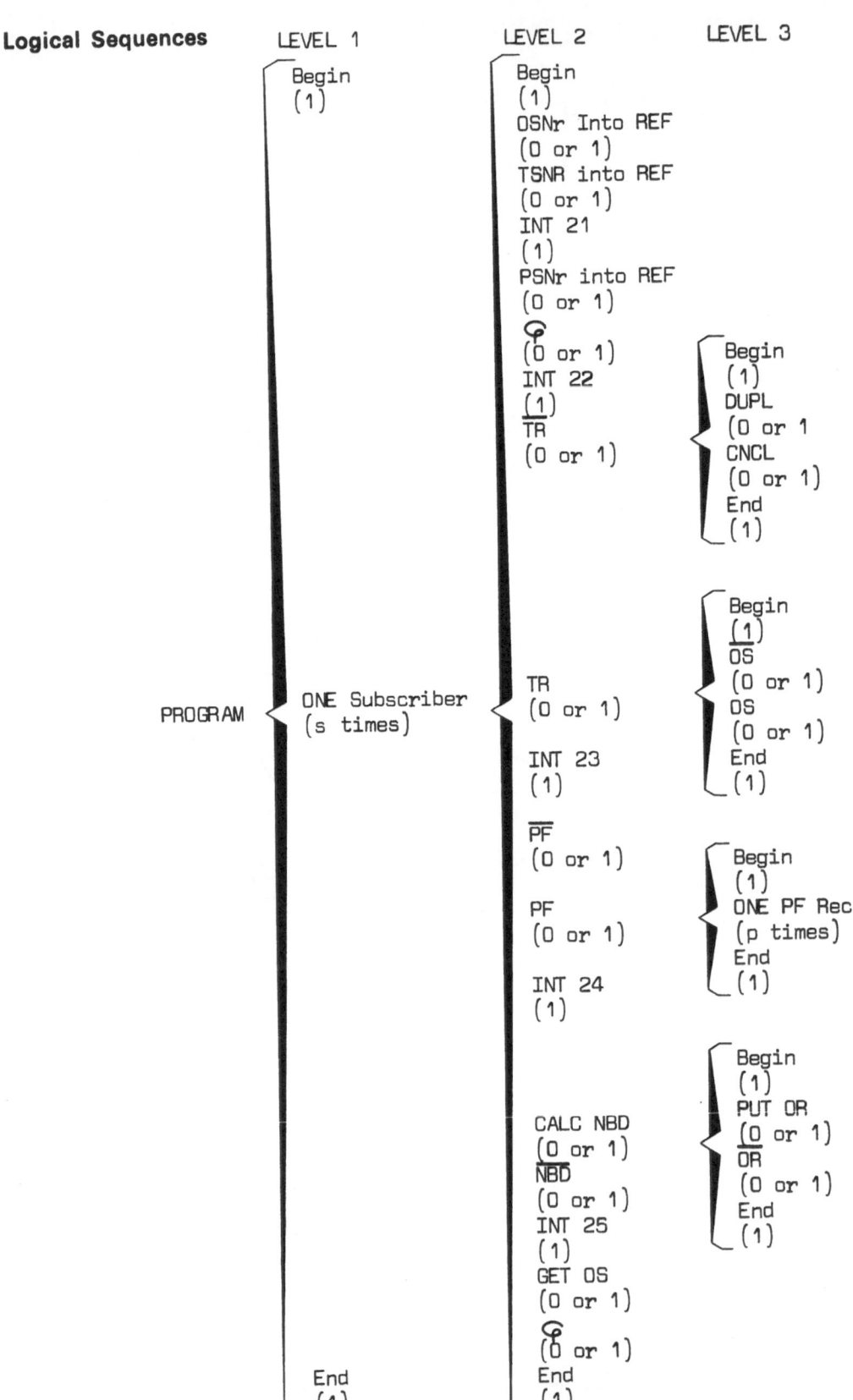

LEVEL 1

Begin
(1)

LEVEL 2

Begin
(1)
OSNr Into REF
(0 or 1)
TSNR into REF
(0 or 1)
INT 21
(1)
PSNr into REF
(0 or 1)
⌐
(0 or 1)
INT 22
(1)
TR
(0 or 1)

LEVEL 3

Begin
(1)
DUPL
(0 or 1
CNCL
(0 or 1)
End
(1)

PROGRAM

ONE Subscriber
(s times)

TR
(0 or 1)

INT 23
(1)

Begin
(1)
OS
(0 or 1)
OS
(0 or 1)
End
(1)

PF
(0 or 1)

PF
(0 or 1)

INT 24
(1)

Begin
(1)
ONE PF Rec
(p times)
End
(1)

CALC NBD
(0 or 1)
NBD
(0 or 1)
INT 25
(1)
GET OS
(0 or 1)
⌐
(0 or 1)
End
(1)

Begin
(1)
PUT OR
(0 or 1)
OR
(0 or 1)
End
(1)

End
(1)

End
(1)

Flowchart to Level 3.

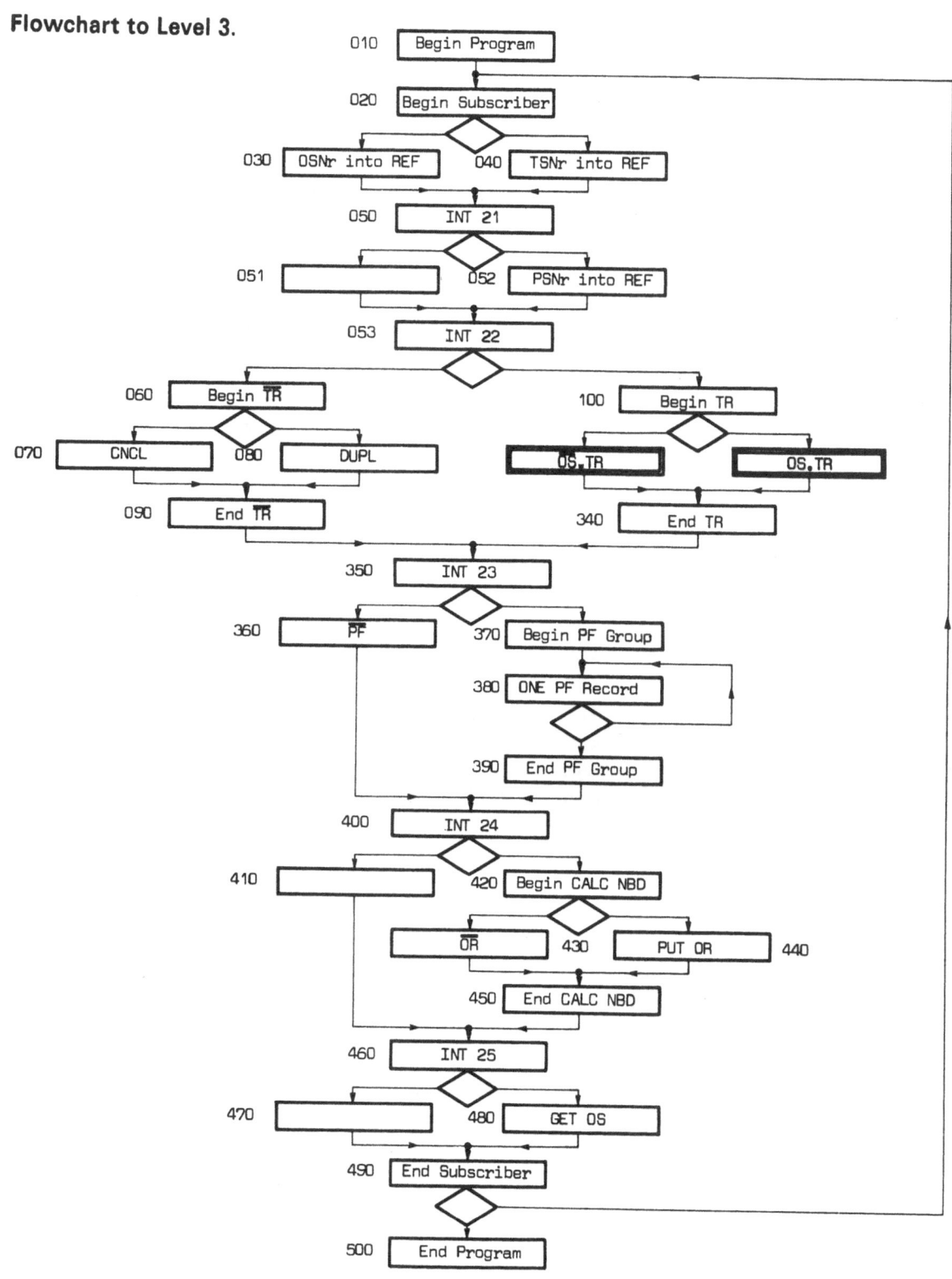

Now perform the detailed organization of the program, and check it against the LOF before looking at the proposed solution that follows.

Instructions to be added

010	GET OS		
010	GET TR		
010	GET PF		
480	GET OS		
340	GET TR		
380	GET PF		
020	IF TSNr $<$ OSNr		040
030			050
050	IF PSNr $<$ REFNr		052
051			053
053	IF TSNr = REFNr		100

branches unchanged to seq. 350

350	IF PSNr = REFNr		370
360			400
380	IF PSNr = REFNr		380
400	IF N = 1		420
410			460
420	IF NBD $<$ 0		440
430			450
460	IF OSNr = REFNr		480
470			490
490	IF $\overline{\text{EOF}}$		020

add to branch-preparation routines:

052	PSNr into REF
020	N = 0
080	N = 1
120	N = 1
260	N = 1
330	OBD into CAL
090	OBD into CAL
350	ΣAP = 0
380	ΣAP + AP
420	CAL $-$ ΣAP
420	FMT NBD from CAL
420	PUT NS
440	FMT OR Rec
440	PUT OR & INIT

Sequenced list of instructions

010	GET OS		260	FMT TR Rec into NS	
	GET TR			$N = 1$	
	GET PF			PUT NS	310
020	$N = 0$		270	FMT ESNr, ENA	
	IF TSNr $<$ OSNr	040		IF C $\neq$ 2	290
030	OSNr into REF	050	280	FMT Create–MSG	300
040	TSNr into REF		290	FMT Code–MSG	
050	IF PSNr $=$ REFNr	052	300	PUT ER & INIT	
051		053	310		
052	PSNr into REF		320		
053	IF TSNr $=$ REFNr	100	330	OBD into CAL	
060	IF OED $>$ CD	080	340	GET TR	
070	Cancel NS		350	$\Sigma AP = 0$	
080	$N = 1$			IF PSNr $=$ REFNr	370
090	OBD into CAL	350	360		400
100	IF OSNr $=$ REFNr	210	370		
110	IF C $\neq$ 2	130	380	$\Sigma AP + AP$	
120	$N = 1$			GET PF	
	FMT NS Rec			IF PSNr $=$ REFNr	380
	PUT NS	200	390		
130	FMT ESNr, ENA		400	IF $N = 1$	420
	IF C $\neq$ 0	150	410		460
140	FMT Cancel–MSG	190	420	CAL — ΣAP	
150	IF C $=$ 1	170		FMT NBD from CAL	
160	FMT Code–MSG	180		PUT NS	
170	FMT Alter–MSG			IF NBD $<$ 0	440
180			430		450
190	PUT ER and INIT		440	FMT OR Rec	
200		340		PUT OR and INIT	
210	IF TED $<$ CD	230	450		
220	Cancel NS	330	460	IF OSNr $=$ REFNr	480
230	IF C $\neq$ 0	250	470		490
240	Cancel NS	320	480	GET OS	
250	IF C $\neq$ 1	270	490	IF $\overline{EOF}$	020
			500	END	

4 — PAYROLL

SIMPLIFIED PAYROLL PROBLEM

All the personnel of a given company's office in country X are salaried. The problem is to calculate and print monthly pay slips for the office.

Program Diagram

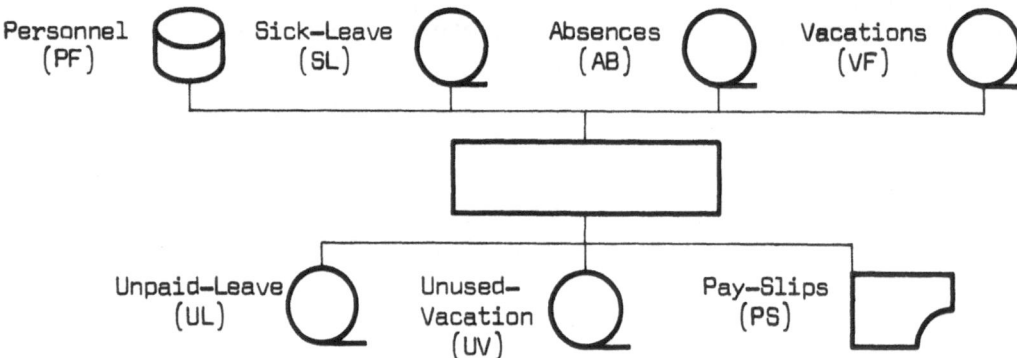

Outputs

Pay-Slip (PS) format.

To simplify the description of the various records in PS, the number-of-times value for each item (1 or 0/1) is given. Values given in quotation marks are to appear on the form.

Date (D) 1	Name (N) 1	Social-Security No (SS) 1
	Address (ADR) 1	Employee-No (ENr) 1
	City-State-Zip (CSZ) 1	Job-Title (JT) 1

"GROSS SALARY" (GS) 1		GS-Amount (GSA) 1
"LESS ABSENCES" (LA) 0/1	LA-Amount (LAA) 0/1	
"LESS SICK LEAVE" (LS) 0/1	SL-Amount (LSA) 0/1	
"SICK PAY" (SP) 0/1		SP-Amount (SPA) 1
"LESS VACATION" (LV) 0/1	LV-Amount (LVA) 0/1	
"VACATION PAY" (VP) 0/1		VP-Amount (VPA) 0/1
"SUBTOTAL" (ST) 1		ST-Amount (STA) 1
"BASIC SOCIAL SECURITY" (BS) 0/1	BS-Amount (BSA) 0/1	
"EXTRA SOCIAL SECURITY" (ES) 0/1	ES-Amount (ESA) 0/1	
"TAXABLE SALARY" (TS) 1		TS-Amount (TSA) 1
"UNITED FUND" (UF) 0/1	UF-Amount (UFA) 0/1	
"NET PAY" (NP) 1		NP-Amount (NPA) 1

In country X, there is no 'withholding tax' or PAYE system, so the company has no tax calculations to perform aside from determining the value of TSA. On the other hand, the national Social Security system in country X partially compensates employers for sick pay; the calculations involved are described below.

Unpaid-Leave (UL) format (0 or 1 record per employee).

Employee-No (ULNr)	Days-Absent (Σ DA)

There is a record for each employee having LAA > 0; also, if the number of days vacation taken exceeds that allowed, the difference is added to the Σ DA value.

Unused-Vacation (UV) format (0 or 1 record per employee).

Employee-No (UVNr)	Paid-Days-Remaining (PD)	Allowed-Days-Remaining (AD)

There is a record for each employee who still has vacation time owed by the company (AD > 0). If he takes some vacation during the month, there is an LV entry on the pay slip, and the number of days taken is deducted from AD. If AD is zero, the record is written anyway.

INPUTS

Personnel file (PF) format (1 record per employee.)

Employee-No (PNr)	Name (N)	Address (ADR)	City-State-Zip (CSZ)	SS-No (SS)	//—

Job-Title (JT)	Salary (GSA)	Paid-Vacation (PV)	Allowed-Vacation (AV)	Codes X | Y | Z

The value PV indicates the number of days paid vacation to which the employee is still entitled; the value AV indicates the number of days allowed which remain to him, paid or not. Where an employee has been with the company for less than a year, or has vacation time left over from the previous year, the number of days allowed (AV) may exceed the number of days paid (PV).

Codes X and Y indicate the amount of sick pay to which the employee is entitled, as determined by his seniority or by the length of his illness.

$$\overline{X}.\overline{Y} = \quad 0\%$$
$$\overline{X}.Y = \quad 50\%$$
$$X.\overline{Y} = \quad 75\%$$
$$X.Y = 100\%$$

where the percentage is the amount paid by the company of the difference between the Social Security sick pay allowance and the employee's normal salary.

X will be another way of writing that code $X = 1$ and X that code $= 1$ (and similarly for Y).

Code Z indicates that the employee makes a contribution to a 'United Fund' organization.

Sick-Leave file (SL) format (0 or 1 record per employee)

Employee-No (SLNr)	Days-Illness (DI)

There is a record where DI > 0 for the month.

Absences file (AB) format (0 or 1 record per employee)

Employee—No (ABNr)	Days—Absent (DA)

There is a record when $DA > 0$ for the month.

Vacation file (VF) format (0 or 1 record per emplyee).

Employee—No (VFNr)	Days—Vacation (DV)

There is a record when $DV > 0$ for the month.

Calculations

Sick Pay (SPA)

- Daily salary (DS) in any month is one-thirtieth the gross salary (GSA).
- The daily payment from Social Security (SSP) is 40% of the daily salary (DS) where this is less than a daily ceiling value (DCV). Where $DS \geqslant DCV$, SSP is 40% of DCV.

- To this is added company sick pay (CSP).
- 50% of the difference (DS – SSP) where $\overline{X}.Y$.
- 75% of the difference where $X.\overline{Y}$.
- 100% of the difference where X.Y.

- The daily total sick pay is multiplied by the number of day's illness to yield Sick-Pay-Amount (SPA):

$$SPA = (SSP + CSP) \times DI$$

Subtotal (STA)

$$STA = GSA - (LAA + LSA + LVA) + (SPA + VPA)$$

Deductions from the gross salary

- Less-Absences-Amount:
$$LAA = DS \times DA$$
- Less-Sick-Leave-Amount:
$$LSA = DS \times DI$$
- Less-Vacation-Amount:
$$LVA = DS \times DV$$

Vacation

- Vacation-Pay-Amount (VPA):
    $T = DA + DV$
    If $T < PV$, then days-paid (DP) $= T$
        and $PD = PV - T$.
    If $T \overline{< PV}$, then $DP = PV$
        and $PD = 0$.
    $VPA = DS \times DP$.
- Allowed-Days-Remaining (AD):
    $AD = AV - T$.
- If $AD \overline{< 0}$, an Unused-Vacation (UV) record is to be produced.
- If $AD < 0$, an Unpaid-Leave (UL) record is to be produced.

Social Security

- A ceiling value (CV) enters into the following calculations. This value is a constant determined by the legislation of country X. The daily ceiling value (DCV) used in sick-pay calculations is one-thirtieth the value CV.
- Calculation of Social Security contributions is based on the subtotal (STA) less any Social Security payments (SSP); we will call the result the Social Security base (SSB):

    $SSB = STA - SSP$.

  Note that the company's payment for sick leave (CSP) is not involved in this calculation.
- Basic Social Security (BSA) contribution:

    If $SSB < CV$, then BSA $= 5.5\%$ of SSB.
    If $SSB \overline{< CV}$, then BSA $= 5.5\%$ of CV.

- Extra Social Security (ESA) contribution:

    $ESA = 1\%$ of SSB.

Taxable-Salary-Amount (TSA):

$TSA = STA - (BSA + ESA)$

United-Fund-Amount (UFA):

If $Z = 1$, UFA $= 1\%$ of TSA.

Net-Pay-Amount (NPA):

If $Z = 1$, NPA = TSA − UFA.
If $Z = 0$, NPA = TSA.

Country X, you may have guessed, resembles France to some degree; but no country follows exactly the formulae given here.

Construct the Logical Output File, and check your result against that given on the next page before continuing.

Logical Output File

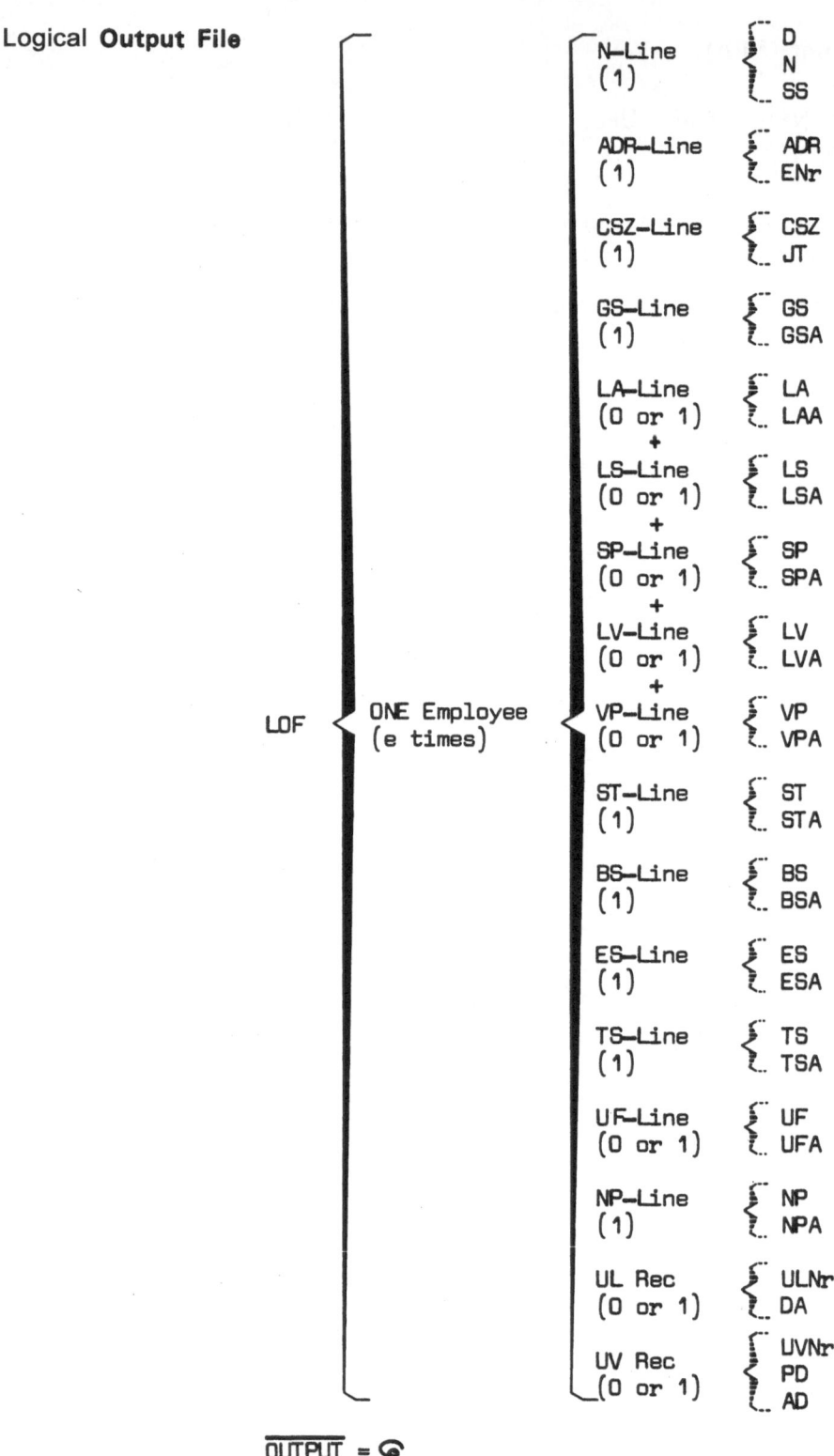

N—Line (1) — D, N, SS

ADR—Line (1) — ADR, ENr

CSZ—Line (1) — CSZ, JT

GS—Line (1) — GS, GSA

LA—Line (0 or 1) — LA, LAA
+
LS—Line (0 or 1) — LS, LSA
+
SP—Line (0 or 1) — SP, SPA
+
LV—Line (0 or 1) — LV, LVA
+
VP—Line (0 or 1) — VP, VPA

ST—Line (1) — ST, STA

BS—Line (1) — BS, BSA

ES—Line (1) — ES, ESA

TS—Line (1) — TS, TSA

UF—Line (0 or 1) — UF, UFA

NP—Line (1) — NP, NPA

UL Rec (0 or 1) — ULNr, DA

UV Rec (0 or 1) — UVNr, PD, AD

LOF — ONE Employee (e times)

$\overline{\text{OUTPUT}}$ = ⌀

Now do the Logical Input File, and any Logical Phase Files that may be needed.

Logical Input File

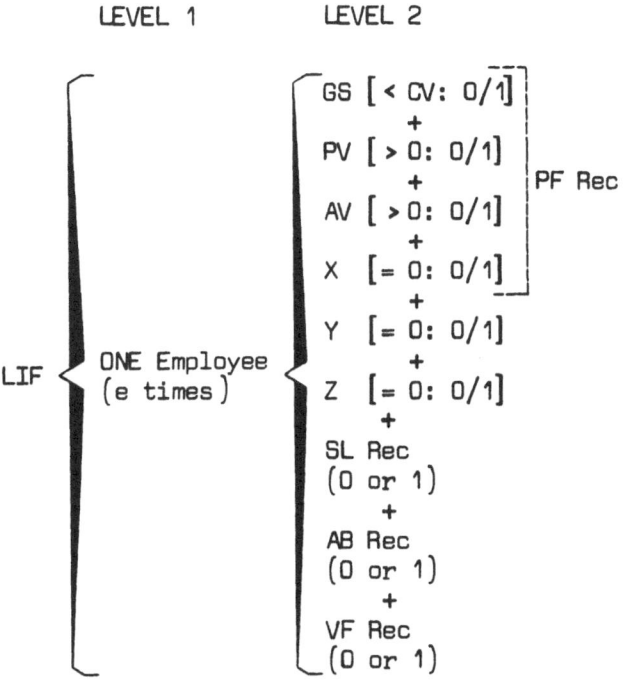

```
                    LEVEL 1         LEVEL 2

                                  ⌈ GS [ < CV: 0/1]  ⌉
                                  |       +          |
                                  | PV [ > 0: 0/1]   |
                                  |       +          | PF Rec
                                  | AV [ > 0: 0/1]   |
                                  |       +          |
                                  | X  [ = 0: 0/1]   ⌋
            ⌈                     |       +
            |                     | Y  [ = 0: 0/1]
            |   ONE Employee      |       +
LIF ⟨       ⟨   (e times )    ⟨   | Z  [ = 0: 0/1]
            |                     |       +
            |                     | SL Rec
            |                     | (0 or 1)
            |                     |       +
            ⌊                     | AB Rec
                                  | (0 or 1)
                                  |       +
                                  | VF Rec
                                  ⌊ (0 or 1)
```

Logical Phase Files

```
                               ⌈ T [ > AV: 0/1]
            ⌈  ONE Employee     |
LPF2  ⟨     ⟨  AB + VF      ⟨   |      +          (where T = DA + DV)
            ⌊                   |
                               ⌊ T [ < PV: 0/1]
```

```
LPF3  ⟨ ONE Employee  ⟨ DP [ > 0: 0/1]
        T > 0
```

```
LPF5  ⟨ ONE Employee  ⟨ SSB [ < CV: 0/1]
```

Now construct the truth table for Level 2, and whatever tables are needed for level 3. Note that the value of the gross salary (GS) and those of codes X and Y are relevant here only if the employee has taken sick leave; and that the number of paid days (PD) and authorized days (AD) are of interest only if the employee has taken paid or unpaid leave during the month. Code Z is independent of all these values.

Table T 1

ONE Employee DI	DA	DV	LA	LS See T2	LV	No Action	CALC T Phase 2
0	0	0				X	
0	1	1			X		X
0	0	0	X				X
0	1	1	X		X		X
1	0	0		X			
1	0	1		X	X		X
1	1	0	X	X			X
1	1	1	X	X	X		X

Table T 2

ONE Employee DI DS<	X	Y	CALC SSP DS < DCV	CALC SSP $\overline{DS < DCV}$	+ 50% of DS − SSP	+ 75% of DS − SSP	+ 100% of DS − SSP
0	0	0		X			
0	0	1		X	X		
0	1	0		X		X	
0	1	1		X			X
1	0	0	X				
1	0	1	X		X		
1	1	0	X			X	
1	1	1	X				X

Where 'DS <' stands for DS < DCV:

Table T 3

ONE Employee T >AV <PV	① DP = T CALC PD	② UL Rec	③ UV Rec	④ See LPF3	⑤ DP = PV AD = 0
0 0			X	X	X
0 1	X		X	X	
1 0		X		X	X
1 1	♀	♀	♀	♀	♀

Where '> AV' stands for T > AV and '< PV' stands for T < PV:

Now subdivide the program into logical sequences. Check your solution against the Logical Output File and the description of the calculations to be performed. Then compare your solution with that proposed on the next page before attempting the logical-sequence flowchart.

Logical Sequences

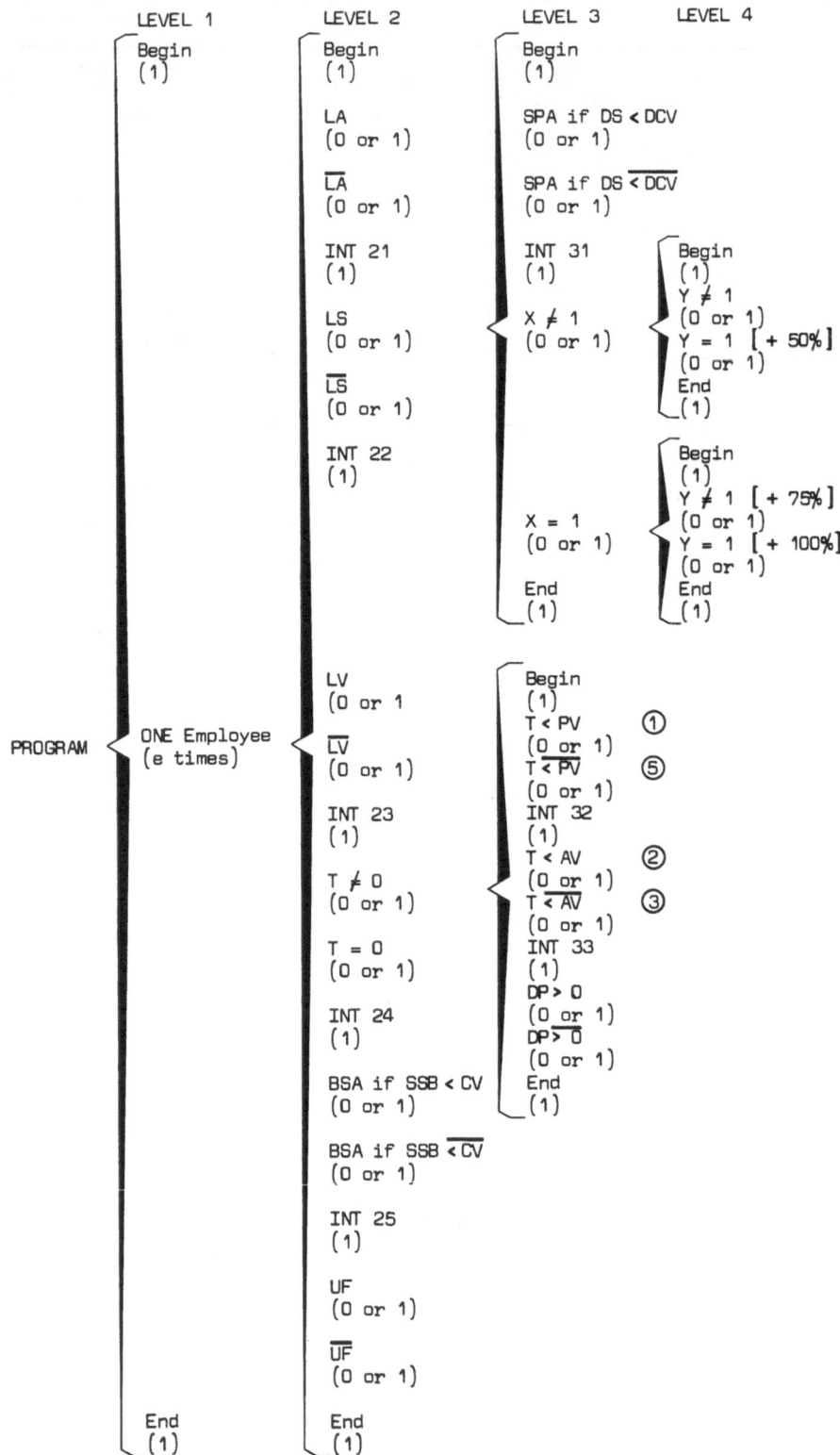

Flowchart of Logical Sequences

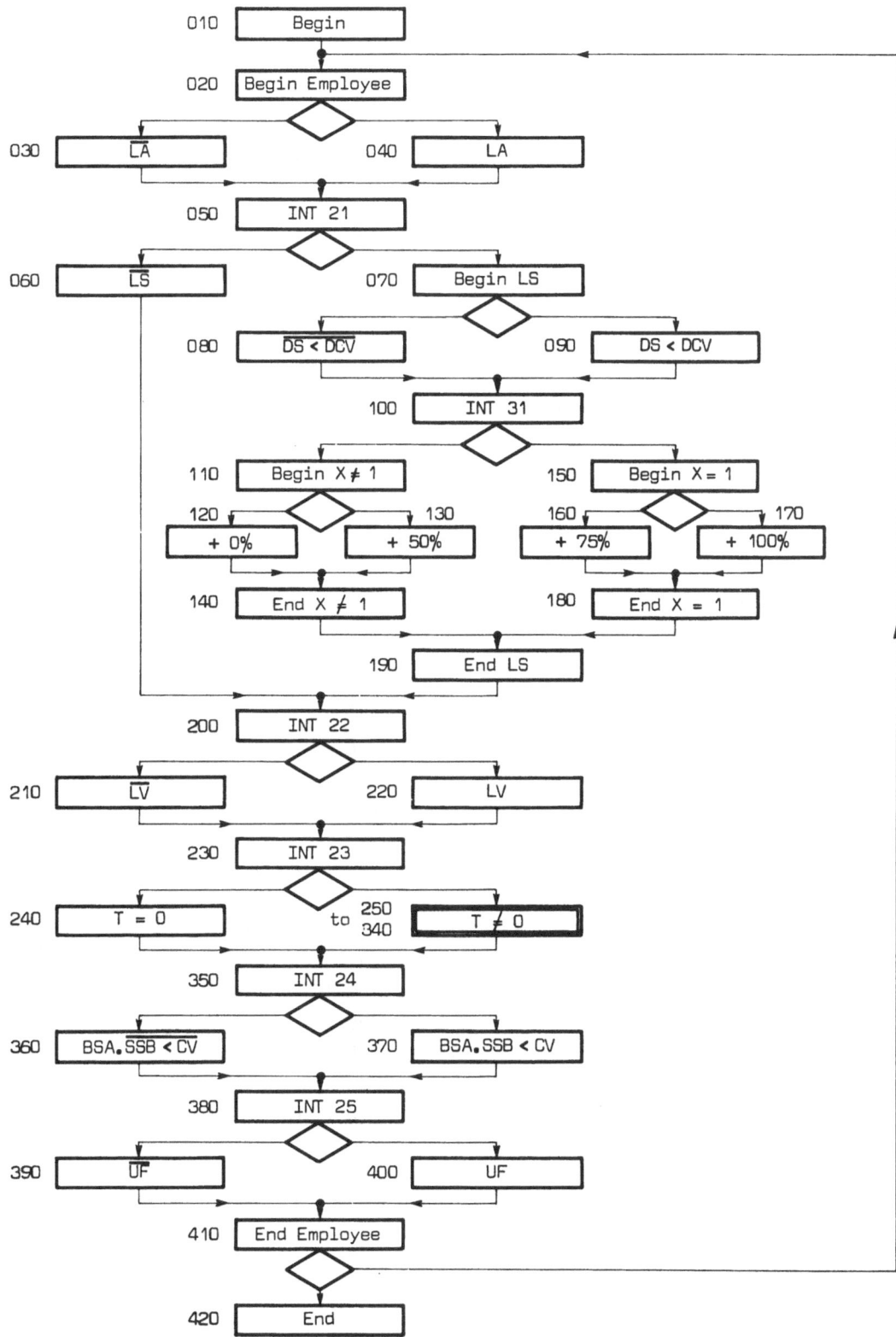

Flowchart for the T ≠ 0 Subset

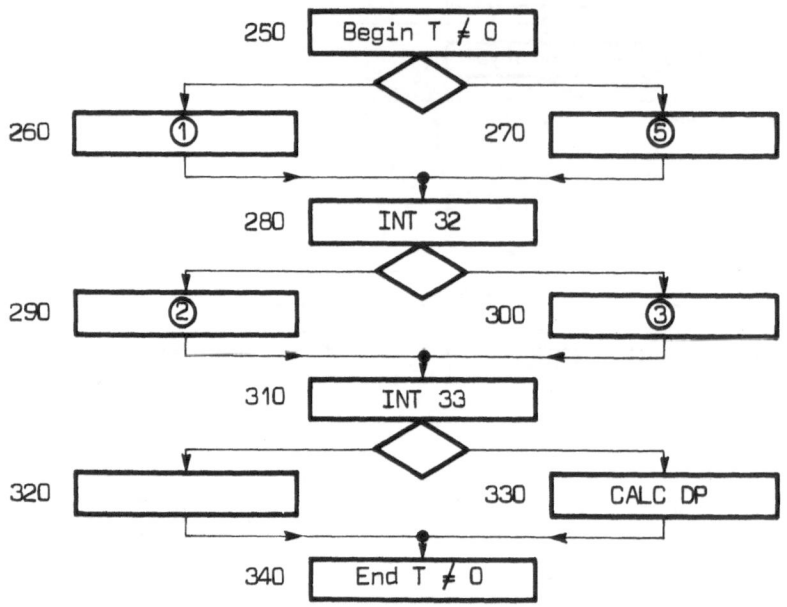

Now write the detailed organization of the program.

List of instructions by category

010 GET PF		
010 GET AB		
010 GET SL		
010 GET VF		
410 GET PF		
040 GET AB		
190 GET SL		
220 GET VF		

020 IF ABNr = PNr	040
030	050
050 IF SLNr = PNr	070
060	200
070 IF DS ⌐ DVC	090
080	100
100 IF X = 1	150
110 IF Y = 1	130

120	140
140	190
150 IF Y = 1	170
160	180
200 IF VFNr = PNr	220
210	230
230 IF T > 0	250
240	350
250 IF T $\overline{<}$ PV	270
260	280
280 IF T $\overline{>}$ AV	300
290	310
310 IF DP > 0	330
320	340
350 IF SSB < CV	370
360	380
380 IF Z = 1	400

390
410 IF $\overline{\text{EOF}}$ 410   400 UFA = TSA × 1%
                                      020   400 NPA = TSA − UFA

020 T = 0   020 FMT N-Line
040 T + DA   020 PUT PS & INIT
220 T + DV   020 FMT ADR-Line
                                                             020 PUT PS & INIT
040 LAA = DS × DA   020 FMT CSZ-Line
070 LSA = DS × DI   020 PUT PS & INIT
220 LVA = DS × DV   020 FMT GS-Line
090 SSP = DS × 40%   020 PUT PS & INIT
080 SSP = DCV × 40%   040 FMT LA-Line
100 ∧ SSP = DS − SSP   040 PUT PS & INIT
130 CSP = ∧ SSP × 50%   070 FMT LS-Line
160 CSP = ∧ SSP × 75%   070 PUT PS & INIT
170 CSP = ∧ SSP   190 FMT SP-Line
190 SPA = (SSP + CSP) × DI   190 PUT PS & INIT
260 DP = T   220 FMT LV-Line
260 AD = DV − T   220 PUT PS & INIT
270 AD = 0   330 FMT VP-Line
270 DP = DV   330 PUT PS & INIT
290 DA = T − AV   350 FMT ST-Line
300 AD = AV − T   350 PUT PS & INIT
330 VPA = DS × DP   380 FMT BS-Line
                                                             380 PUT PS & INIT
020 GSA into CAL   380 FMT ES-Line
040 CAL − LAA   380 PUT PS & INIT
070 CAL − LSA   380 FMT TS-Line
220 CAL − LVA   380 PUT PS & INIT
190 CAL + SPA   400 FMT UF-Line
330 CAL + VPA   400 PUT PS & INIT
350 CAL into WRK   410 FMT NP-Line
350 SSB = STA − (SSP × DI)   410 PUT PS & INIT
370 BSA = SSB × 5.5%
360 BSA = CV × 5.5%   290 FMT UL Rec
380 ESA = SSB × 1%   290 PUT UL
380 SA = BSA + ESA   300 FMT UV Rec
380 TSA = WRK − SA   300 PUT UV

Sequenced list of instructions

Line	Instruction	Jump		Line	Instruction	Jump
010	GET PF			150	IF Y = 1	170
	GET AB			160	CSP = $\triangle$ SSP × 75%	180
	GET SL			170	CSP = $\triangle$ SSP	
	GET VF			180		
020	T = 0			190	SPA = (SSP + CSP) × DI	
	GSA into CAL				CAL + SPA	
	FMT N-Line				FMT SP-Line	
	PUT PS & INIT				PUT PS & INIT	
	FMT ADR-Line				GET SL	
	PUT PS & INIT			200	IF VFNr = PNr	220
	FMT CSZ-Line			210		230
	PUT PS & INIT			220	T + DV	
	FMT GS–Line				LVA = DS × DV	
	PUT PS & INIT				CAL — LVA	
	IF ABNr = PNr	040			FMT LV-Line	
030		050			PUT PS & INIT	
040	T + DA				GET VF	
	LAA = DS × DA			230	IF T > 0	250
	CAL — LAA			240		350
	FMT LA-Line			250	IF T < PV	270
	PUT PS & INIT			260	DP = T	
	GET AB				AD = DV — T	280
050	IF SLNr = PNr	070		270	DP = PV	
060		200			AD = 0	
070	LSA = DS × DI			280	IF T > AV	300
	CAL — LSA			290	DA = T — AV	
	FMT LS-Line				FMT UL Rec	
	PUT PS & INIT				PUT UL	310
	IF DS < DCV	090		300	AD = AV — T	
080	SSP = DCV × 40%	100			FMT UV Rec	
090	SSP = DS × 40%				PUT UV	
100	$\triangle$ SSP = DS — SSP			310	IF DP > 0	330
	IF X = 1	150		320		340
110	IF Y = 1	130		330	VPA = DS × DP	
120	CSP = 0	140			FMT VP-Line	
130	CSP = $\triangle$ SSP × 50%				PUT PS & INIT	
140		190		340	CAL + VPA	

350	CAL into WRK			PUT PS & INIT	
	SSB = STA — (SSP × DI)			FMT TS-Line	
	FMT ST-Line			PUT PS & INIT	
	PUT PS & INIT			IF Z = 1	400
	IF SSB < CV	370	390		410
360	BSA = CV × 5.5%	380	400	UFA = TSA × 1%	
				NPA = TSA — UFA	
370	BSA = SSB × 5.5%			FMT UF-Line	
380	ESA = SSB × 1%			PUT PS & INIT	
	SA = BSA + ESA		410	FMT NP-Line	
	TSA = WRK — SA			PUT PS & INIT	
	FMT BS-Line			GET PF	
	PUT PS & INIT			IF $\overline{EOF}$	020
	FMT ES-Line		420		END

MODIFICATION 1

It is required that annually, in December, the basic Social Security payments for the year be adjusted. In the course of the year it may well happen that the salary on which these payments are based (SSB) may be less than the Social Security ceiling value (CV); or that the ceiling itself may be changed.

Calculations

- For the twelve months of the year:

$$\Sigma CV = (CV\,1 + CV\,2 + CV\,3 \ldots CV\,12)$$
$$\Sigma SSB = (SSB\,1 + SSB\,2 + SSB\,3 \ldots SSB\,12)$$
$$\Sigma BSA = (BSA\,1 + BSA\,2 + BSA\,3 \ldots BSA\,12) \times 5.5$$

- The difference (BDIF) between the total ceiling values and the total of salaries used to calculate the basic Social Security payments:

$$BDIF = \Sigma CV - \Sigma BSA.$$

- Where BDIF > 0, calculate ceiling difference (CDIF):

$$CDIF = \Sigma CV - \Sigma SSB$$

- If CDIF < 0, calculate the adjustment (SSA):

$$SSA = BDIF \times 5.5\%$$

- If CDIF $\overline{< 0}$ and $(\Sigma SSB - \Sigma BSA) > 0$:

     $SSA = (\Sigma SSB - \Sigma BSA) \times 5.5\%$

- For the month of December, calculation of the taxable salary (TSA) is modified:

     $TSA = GS - (BSA + ESA + SSA)$.

Output

A new line is added to Pay Slip file, ahead of the TSA line.

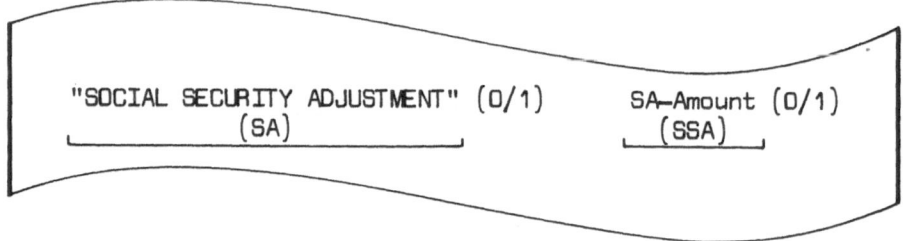

Input

The following fields are added to the **Personnel file (PF)** record.

Month—No (MON)	Total—Ceiling (Σ CV)	Total—Base (Σ SSB)	Total—Basic—Payment (Σ BSA)

Modify the logical output and input files. Are there new processing phases? If so, describe the logical phase files, modify the set of logical sequences P1 and the flowchart (if needed). Check your solution against ours before proceeding.

We give here only those parts of the program documentation which are modified. But recall that in a working environment it is essential that the documentation for a modified program be just as clear and as complete as that for the original program. This is required for any subsequent modifications.

Logical Output File

```
                                    ┌ Unchanged through
                                    │ ES—Line
                                    │
         LOF ┤ ONE Employee ┤ SA—Line      ┌ SA  (1)
             │ (e times)      (0 or 1)     ┤ SSA (1)
                                    │
                                    │ Unchanged from
                                    └ TS—Line
```

Logical Input File

$$\text{LIF} \left\{ \begin{array}{l} \text{ONE Employee} \\ \text{(e times)} \end{array} \right. \left\{ \text{MON} \; [=12: \; 0/1] \quad \text{inserted into PF Rec} \right.$$

Logical Phase Files

$$\text{LPF4} \left\{ \text{ONE Employee} \left\{ \text{BDIF} \; [>0: \; 0/1] \left\{ \begin{array}{ll} \text{CDIF} \; [<0: \; 0/1] & \text{(C--condition)} \\ \quad + \\ (\Sigma\text{SSB} - \Sigma\text{BSA}) \; [>0: \; 0/1] & \text{(D--condition)} \end{array} \right. \right. \right.$$

Truth table for phase 4, level 2:

BDIF > 0 C D	CALC SSA from BDIF	CALC SSA from (ΣSSB− ΣBSA)	NO SSA
0 0			X
0 1		X	
1 0	X		
1 1	X		

Logical Sequences

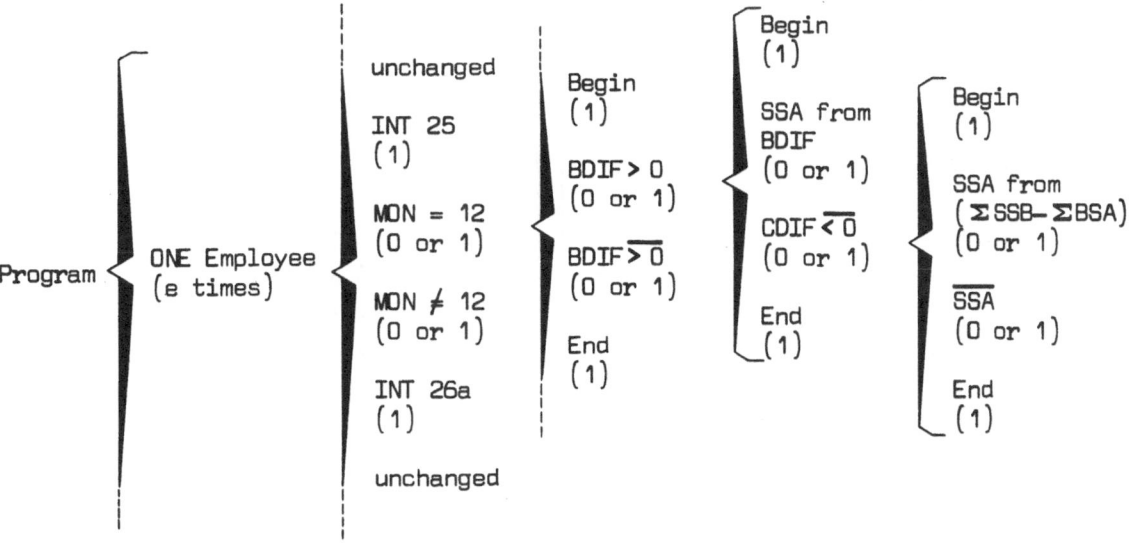

Flowchart

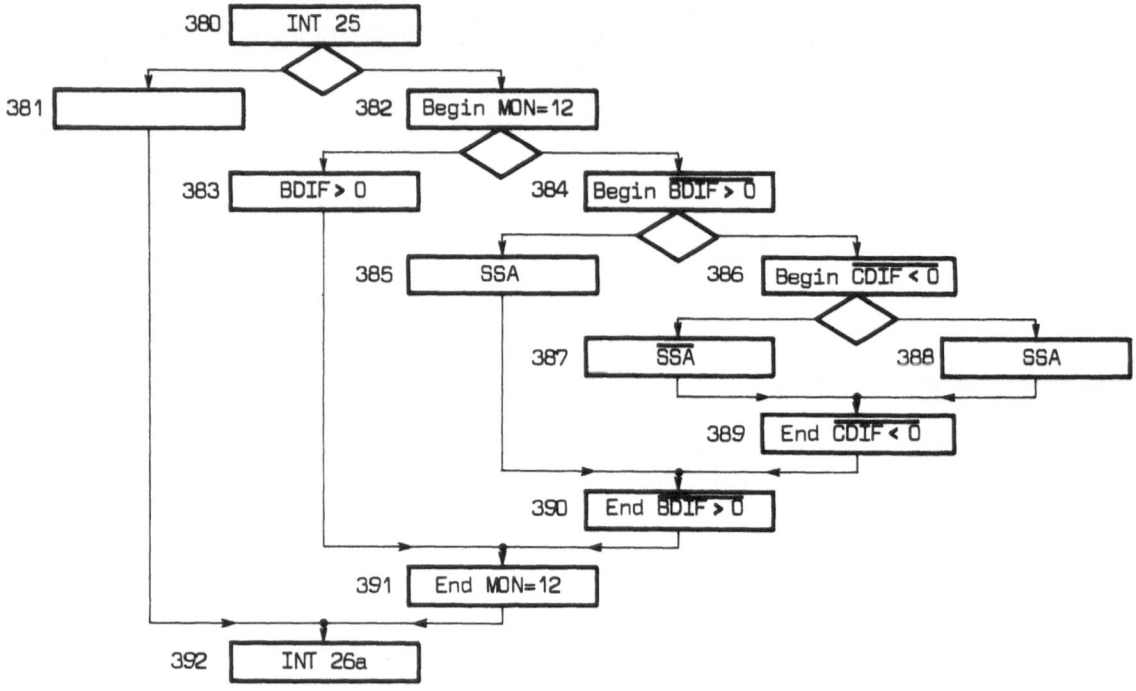

The logical sequence numbered 390 in the original program now becomes sequence 393.

Now write the detailed organization of the modified part of the program, and then list the instructions in order for sequences 380 to 392.

List of Instructions by category

380 IF MON = 12	382	
381	392	
382 IF BDIF > 0	384	
383	391	
384 IF CDIF $\overline{< 0}$	386	
385	390	
386 IF (ΣSSB – ΣBSA) > 0	388	
387	389	
392 IF Z = 1	400	
393	410	
382 ΣCV + CV		
382 ΣSSB + SSB		
382 ΣBSA + BSA		

384 CDIF = ΣCV — ΣSSB
382 BDIF = ΣCV — ΣBSA
385 SSA = (ΣSSB — ΣBSA) × 5.5%
388 SSA = BDIF × 5.5%
390 TSA = GS – (BSA + ESA + SSA)

385 FMT SA-Line
385 PUT PS & INIT
388 FMT SA-Line
388 PUT PS & INIT

It is equally valid to place the printing of SSA in a subroutine called from sequences 385 and 388. The subroutine would then contain the following instructions:

    S/R FMR SA-Line
        PUT PS & INIT

In the ordered list which follows, note that the instructions of the old sequence 380 have been divided between the new sequences 380 and 392.

Sequenced Instruction List

Taking the solution without subroutine:

380	ESA = SSB × 1%		385	SSA = (ΣSSB — ΣBSA) × 5.5%	
	SA = BSA + ESA			FMT SA-Line	
	TSA = WRK — SA			PUT PS & INIT	390
	FMT BS-Line		386	IF (ΣSSB — ΣBSA) > 0	388
	PUT PS & INIT		387		389
	FMT ES-Line		388	SSA = BDIF × 5.5%	
	PUT PS & INIT			FMT SA-Line	
	IF MON = 12	382		PUT PS & INIT	
381		392	389		
382	ΣCV + CV		390	TSA = GS — (BSA + ESA + SSA)	
	ΣSSB + SSB		391		
	ΣBSA + BSA		392	FMT TS-Line	
	BDIF = ΣCV — ΣBSA			PUT PS & INIT	
	IF BDIF > 0	384		IF Z = 1	400
383		391	393		410
384	CDIF = ΣCV — ΣSSG		400	(rest of the program)	
	IF CDIF < 0	386			

MODIFICATION 2

New modifications have been requested in the payroll program.

* A sequential file, **Sums (SF),** is to be produced, with 0 or 1 record per employee, 1 if MON = 12. Its format:

Employee—No (SFNr)	Total—Ceiling (TCV)	Total—Base (TSSB)	Total—Basic—Payment (TBSA)

  The file will be used to update the Personnel file (PF).
* A new line is to be added to the payslip, ahead of the NP line.

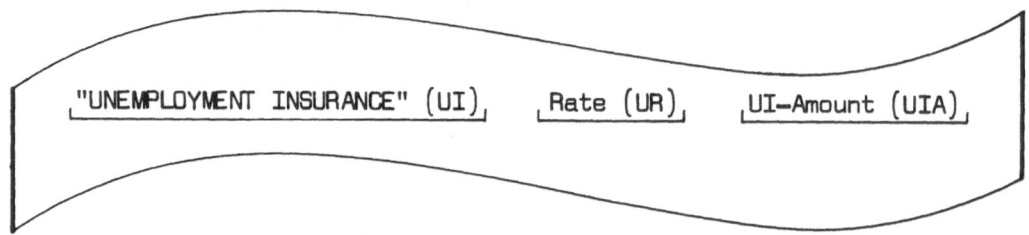

"UNEMPLOYMENT INSURANCE" (UI),   Rate (UR),   UI—Amount (UIA),

The insurance payment is 0.2% of the taxable salary TA, and is to be deducted from the net-pay amount NPA.

Calculations

* Total-Ceiling (TCV):

    $$TCV = \Sigma CV + CV$$

* Total-Base (TSSB):

    $$TSSB = \Sigma SSB + SSB$$

* Total-Basic-Payment (TBSA):

    $$TBSA = \Sigma BSA + BSA$$

Modify the logical output file and see that needed changes are made in the logical input and phase files.

Logical Output File

Again, we show only the modifications.

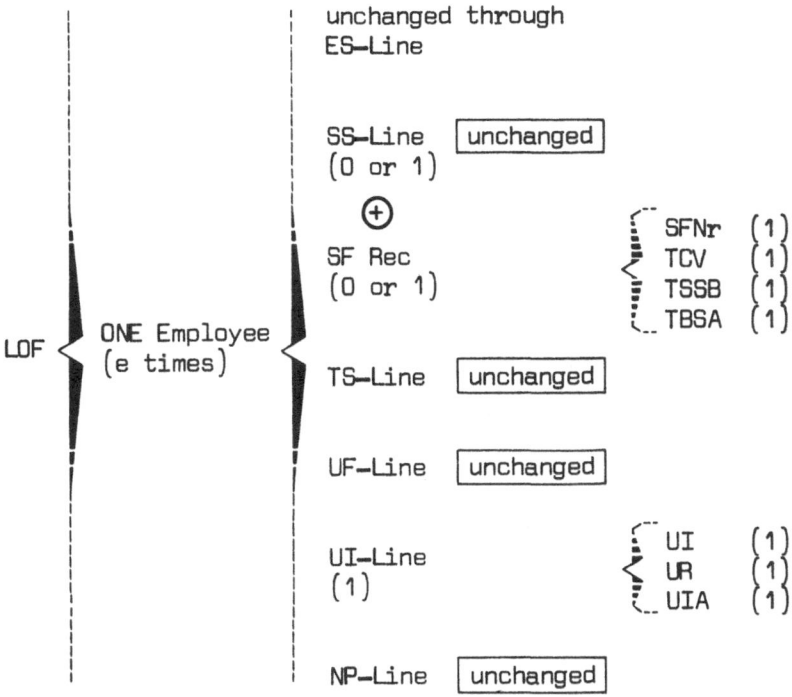

The set of logical sequences P1 is unchanged.

- The set MON ≠ 12 corresponds to sequence 381, in which the SF record is to be produced.
- The UI-Line is to be produced once per employee after the alternative structure which calculates the optional United Fund payment (UFA), i.e. in sequence 410.
- Deduction of the insurance payment UIA to obtain the net amount NPA is also performed in sequence 410, before formatting NP-Line and after calculating UIA.

List of Instructions by Category

381 TCV = ΣCV + CV	381 FMT SFNr
381 TSSB = ΣSSB + SSB	381 FMT TCV
381 TBSA = ΣBSA + BSA	381 FMT TSSB
410 UIA = TSA × 0.2%	381 FMT TBSA
410 NPA – UIA	381 PUT SF
	410 FMT UI-Line
	410 PUT PS & INIT

Sequenced list of instructions

381	TCV = ΣCV + CV	
	TSSB = ΣSSB + SSB	
	TBSA = ΣBSA + BSA	
	FMT SFNr	
	FMT TCV	
	FMT TSSB	
	FMT TBSA	
	PUT SF	392
410	UIA = TSA × 0.2%	
	NPA − UIA	
	FMT UI-Line	
	PUT PS & INIT	
	FMT NP-Line	
	PUT PS & INIT	
	GET PF	
	IF $\overline{EOF}$	020

5 — CONCLUSION

We believe the preceding problems provide some basic themes the teacher can use in developing new exercises, simplifying or complicating the problems posed to the student.

It must be emphasized that in the beginning stages of a course in the logic of program construction, it is absolutely essential that students be given much simpler exercises, of the type found in the two volumes of the book 'Entraînement à la Programmation'.

Finally, we would like to underline the importance of working out the exercises and correcting them step by step: if the student's solution is wrong from the LOF and he waits till the end of the solution before correcting the error, no one whose solution differs from that of the instructor will be able tell what errors he has made. The work done is likely to be wasted effort.

LIST OF ABBREVIATIONS

Abbreviations used throughout the book

CAL	Calculation area
CALC	Calculate value
CNCL	Cancel input record from output
DUPL	Duplicate input record in output
EOF	End of file condition
FMT	Format record/field
INIT	Initialize record/field
INT	Intermediate sequence
LCP	Logical Construction of Programs
LIF	Logical Input File
LOF	Logical Output File
LPF	Logical Phase File
Pi	The set of instructions in a program
PI	The set of logical sequences in a program
Rec	Record
REF	Reference area
S/R	Subroutine
WRK	Work area
$\triangle$	Space or spaces
Σ	Total
$<$	Excluded case
.	'And' in conditions
+	Inclusive 'Or' in conditions/structures
*	Exclusive 'Or' in conditions/structures

Part II Chapter 1: REPORTS AND INPUT CHECKS

ADR	Address in TR record and Invoice
CC	Card Code
CCNr	Current-Customer-No in ER record
CN	Customer-Name in TR record and Invoice
CNr	Customer-Number in TR record and Invoice
CRF	Customer's Reference in TR record and Invoice
CSZ	City-State-Zip in TR record and Invoice
D	Discount of Invoice

DS	Date-Shipped in TR record and Invoice
ECT	Error Counter
ER	Error file card
ERNr	Error-Customer-No in ER record
FF	Foot of Form of Invoice
HOF	Head of Form of Invoice
IV	Invoice
IVD	Invoice-Date of Invoice
LCT	Line Counter
$N\Sigma T$	Net-Total of Invoice
ONr	Order-Number in TR record and Invoice
PD	Place-of-Delivery in TR record and Invoice
PG	Page-Number
PM	Payment-Method in TR record and Invoice
PN	Product-Name in TR record and Invoice
PNr	Product-Number in TR record and Invoice
Q	Quantity in TR record and Invoice
SD	Shipment-Date in TR record
SNr	Shipment-Number in TR record and Invoice
TP	Total-Price of Invoice
TR	Input file card
TX	Sales-Tax of Invoice
UP	Unit-Price in TR record and Invoice
ΣT	Totals of Invoice
ΣTX	Sales-Tax (Total) of Invoice
%D	%-Discount in TR record and Invoice
%TX	%-Tax in TR record
1ER	First Error Code

Part II Chapter 2: STATISTICS

ADR	Address in Customer Record
BAL	Balance
BAL2	Balance of Report 2
CBAL	Balance in Customer Record
CCNr	Customer Number in Customer Record
CF	Customers File
CN	Customer-Name of Report and Customer Record
CN2	Customer-Name of Report 2
CNr	Customer-Number of Report
CNr2	Customer-Number of Report 2
CR	Value of SG if the value of returns (in dollars) exceeds that of sales

CRF	Customer reference
CTRF	(Customer + Title) Reference
DB	Value of SG if the Customer owes the publisher
ECNr	Customer-Number in Error Report
ER	Error Report
G ΣQC.R	Number of copies returned
G ΣQC.S	Number of copies (of all titles) sold (by all bookstores)
G ΣQT.R	Number of titles for which there were returns whether or not there were sales
G ΣQT.$\overline{R}$	Number of titles with no returns for which there were sales
G ΣQT.S	Number of titles for which there were sales, whether or not there were returns
G ΣQT.$\overline{S}$	Number of titles for which there were returns and no sales
HOF	Heading (Head of Form) of Report
HOF2	Heading of Report 2
LCT	Line Counter
MSG2	No-Sale-Message (of Report 2)
PG	Page-Number
PG2	Page counter of Report 2
QR	Quantity returned during the year (for a title and a customer)
QS	Quantity Sold during the year (for a title and a customer)
RCNr	Customer-Number in Returns Record
RF	Returns File
RQ	Quantity returned per title in Returns Record
RTNr	Title Number in Returns Record
SCNr	Customer Number in Sales Record
SF	Sales File
SG	Litteral in Report indicating whether the balance is due or owed (See DB, CR, ZERO)
SG2	Sign of Report 2 (value DB or space)
SQ	Quantity Sold per title in Sales Record
SR	Statistical Report
STNr	Title Number in Sales Record
T	Group of Titles Indicator (T = 1 if group of sales or group of returns or both for one customer)
TNr	Title-Number of Report and Customer Record
TR	Total-Returns (Dollars) in Returns Record
TRF	Title reference
TS	Total of Sales (Dollars) in Sales Record
ZERO	Value of SG if the Balance is Zero
ΣDBB	Total of Debit Balances
ΣCRB	Total of Credit Balances
ΣQR	Σ Quantity Returned per Customer
ΣQS	Σ Quantity Sold per Customer
ΣTR	Value of returns per Customer (Dollars)

ΣTS   Value of Sales per Customer (Dollars)

Part II   Chapter 3: FILE UPDATE

AP	Amount Paid in Payment Record
C	Code in Transaction Record
CD	Current Date
ENA	Name/Address of Error Report
ER	Error Report
ESNr	Subscription Number of Error Report
MSG	Error-Message
NBD	Balance-Due in New Subscribers Record
NED	Expiration-Date in New Subscribers Record
NNA	Name/Address in New Subscribers Record
NS	New Subscribers
NSD	Subscription-Date in New Subscribers Record
NSNr	Subscription Number in New Subscribers Record
OA	Overpaid Amount
OBD	Balance-Due in Old Subscribers Record
OED	Expiration-Date in Old Subscribers Record
ONA	Name/Address in Old Subscribers Record
OR	Overpayment Report
ORNA	Name/Address of overpayment Report
ORSNr	Subscription-Number of overpayment Report
OS	Old Subscribers
OSD	Subscription-Date in Old Subscribers Record
OSNr	Subscription-Number in Old Subscribers Record
PF	Payment File
PSNr	Subscription Number in Payment Record
TED	Expiration Date in Transaction Record
TNA	Name/Address in Transaction Record
TR	Transactions
TSD	Subscription Date in Transaction Record
TSNr	Subscription Number in Transaction Record
ΣAP	Total Amount per Subscription

Part II   Chapter 4: PAYROLL

AB	Absences File
ABNr	Employee Number of Absences Record
AD	Allowed-Days-Remaining of Unused Vacation Record
ADR	Address in Personnel Record and Pay Slip

AV	Allowed-Vacation of Personnel Record (Days)
BDIF	$\Sigma CV - \Sigma BSA$
BS	'BASIC SOCIAL SECURITY' in Pay Slip
BSA	Basic Social Security, Amount of Pay Slip
CDIF	$\Sigma CV - \Sigma SSB$
CSP	Company-Sick-Pay
CSZ	City-State-Zip in Personnel Record and Pay Slip
CV	Social Security Ceiling Value
D	Date in Personnel Record and Pay Slip
DA	Days of Absence of Absences Record
DCV	Daily Social Security Ceiling Value
DI	Days of Illness of Sick-Leave Record
DP	Days-Paid in calculating VPA
DS	Daily Salary
DV	Days of vacation of Vacation Record
ENr	Employee Number of Pay Slip
ES	'EXTRA SOCIAL SECURITY' in Pay Slip
ESA	Extra Social Security Amount of Pay Slip
GS	'GROSS SALARY' in Pay Slip
GSA	Gross Salary Amount in Personnel Record and Pay Slip
JT	Job-Title in Personnel Record and Pay Slip
LA	'LESS ABSENCES' in Pay Slip
LAA	'LESS ABSENCES' Amount of Pay Slip
LS	'LESS SICK LEAVE' in Pay Slip
LSA	'LESS SICK LEAVE' Amount of Pay Slip
LV	'LESS VACATION' in Pay Slip
LVA	'LESS VACATION' Amount of Pay Slip
MON	Month-Number in Personnel Record
N	Name in Personnel Record and Pay Slip
NP	'NET PAY' in Pay Slip
NPA	Net Pay Amount of Pay Slip
PD	Paid-Days-Remaining of Unused Vacation Record
PF	Personnel File
PS	Pay-Slips
PNr	Employee Number of Personnel Record
PV	Paid Vacation in Personnel Record
SA	'SOCIAL SECURITY ADJUSTMENT' in Pay Slip
SF	Sums File
SL	Sick-Leave File
SFNr	Employee Number of Sums Record
SLNr	Employee Number of Sick-Leave Record
SP	'SICK PAY' in Pay Slip

SPA	Sick Pay Amount of Pay Slip
SS	Social-Security-Number in Personnel Record and Pay Slip
SSA	SS-Adjustment-Amount in PS Record
SSB	Social Security Base (SSB = STA − SSP)
SSP	Daily Social-Security-Sick-Pay
ST	'SUBTOTAL' in Pay Slip
STA	Subtotal of Pay Slip
T	Total Days away from work (T= DA + DV)
TBSA	Total-Basic-Payment of Sums Record
TCV	Total-Ceiling-Value of Sums Record
TS	'TAXABLE SALARY' in Pay Slip
TSA	Taxable Salary Amount of Pay Slip
TSSB	Total-SS-Base of Sums Record
UF	'UNITED FUND' in Pay Slip
UFA	United Fund Amount of Pay-Slip
UI	'UNEMPLOYMENT INSURANCE' in Pay Slip
UIA	Unemployment-Insurance-Amount of Pay-Slip
UL	Unpaid-Leave File
ULNr	Employee Number of Unpaid-Leave Record
UR	Unemployment-Insurance Rate
UV	Unused-Vacation File
UVNr	Employee Number of Unused-Vacation Record
VF	Vacation File
VFNr	Employee Number of Vacation Record
VP	'VACATION PAY' in Pay Slip
VPA	'VACATION PAY' Amount of Pay Slip
ΣBSA	Total of Basic Social Security Amount for the twelve months of the year
ΣCV	Total of Ceiling Value for Social Security for the twelve months of the year
ΣDA	Days of Absence of Unpaid-Leave Record
ΣSSB	Total of Social Security Base for the twelve months of the year